STEALING THE FIRE

STEALING THE FIRE

The Art and Protest of
James Baldwin

HORACE A. PORTER

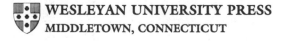 WESLEYAN UNIVERSITY PRESS
MIDDLETOWN, CONNECTICUT

Quotations from *Notes of a Native Son,* by James Baldwin (Copyright © 1955, renewed 1983 by James Baldwin), are reprinted by permission of Beacon Press. Quotations from the following books by James Baldwin are reprinted by permission of The Dial Press: *The Fire Next Time* (Copyright © 1963, 1962 by James Baldwin); *Giovanni's Room* (Copyright © 1956 by James Baldwin); *Going to Meet the Man* (Copyright © 1965 by James Baldwin); *Go Tell It on the Mountain* (Copyright © 1953, 1952 by James Baldwin); *Nobody Knows My Name* (Copyright © 1961 by James Baldwin).

The lines from "(What Did I Do To Be So) Black and Blue," by Andy Razaf, Thomas Waller, and Harry Brooks (Copyright © 1929 by Mills Music Inc.) are reprinted by permission of Mills Music Inc.

All inquiries and permissions requests should be addressed to the Publisher, Wesleyan University Press, 110 Mt. Vernon Street, Middletown, Connecticut 06457

LIBRARY OF CONGRESS CATALOGING-IN-PUBLICATION DATA
Porter, Horace A., 1950–
    Stealing the fire.
    Bibliography: p.
    Includes index.
    1. Baldwin, James, 1924–87—Criticism and
interpretation.   1. Title.
PS3552.A45Z85   1989   818'.5409   88-27806
ISBN 0-8195-5197-X

Manufactured in the United States of America

FIRST EDITION

To Carla Carr

I'm white—inside;
it don't help my case,
'Cause I can't hide—
What is on my face, ooh! . . .
How will it end,
ain't got a friend,
My only sin,
is in my skin—
What did I do,
to be so black and blue?

"Black and Blue"
—Andy Razaf, Thomas Waller, Harry Brooks

One of the attributes, perhaps, of what is taken to be a "healthy" culture, has, generally, and, I suspect, necessarily, a much lower level of tolerance for the maverick, the dissenter, the man who steals the fire, than have societies in which, the common ground of belief having all but vanished, each man, in awful and brutal isolation, is for himself to flower or to perish.

—James Baldwin, "Princes and Powers"

CONTENTS

PREFACE

This book, excluding some final copy and minor revisions, was approaching the production stage when James Baldwin died on December 1, 1987. December was the month I had promised myself and my editor I would deliver the final pages. Then I heard the sad news. Friends and colleagues urged me to speed up. I vacillated between the desire for quick publication and the appropriate manner in which to account for the end of Baldwin's complex life and literary career. It seemed foolish to start over and produce the authoritative and comprehensive interpretation of his life and work. I had decided early on to leave that task to others. My goal was more modest.

This book was inspired by my dissertation, which I completed at Yale. It was directed by Charles T. Davis. I certainly wish, selfishly, that Charlie were still around to see the fruit of his labor and faith and, of course, of mine. The dissertation now seems like something that happened a long time ago in a galaxy far, far away, but after completing it, I had planned simply to "revise" it and rush it to an eager, distinguished university press; so ran the dream. I failed, after several valiant attempts, to revise or indeed revive it; so, excluding a few pages borrowed from my dissertation, this book is entirely new.

Focusing on Baldwin's earliest essays and novels, especially

Notes of a Native Son, Go Tell It on the Mountain, and *Giovanni's Room,* I provide a reinterpretation of James Baldwin's genesis as a writer. Although I make occasional use of crucial biographical details, the study is hardly biographical. Nor is it a full-scale critical study of Baldwin's twenty-two books, of his entire career. My perceptions and insights are drawn from the body of Baldwin's work, ranging from his earliest essays and reviews published during the late 1940s to an address delivered to the National Press Club in December 1986, but, except by implication and in brief allusions, I do not go beyond *The Fire Next Time,* published in 1963.

I look at Baldwin's vocational genesis especially through the lens of literary relationship and influence. I try to discuss both how and why Richard Wright, Harriet Beecher Stowe, and Henry James are significant points of reference for Baldwin. In the prologue, I provide some personal notes on my interest in Baldwin's work. The introduction considers Baldwin in relation to the Afro-American literary tradition of social protest, and his ambivalence toward that tradition. The first chapter discusses *Notes of a Native Son,* Baldwin's early attempt to focus his literary vision. The chapters that follow focus on Baldwin's ambivalent relation to Stowe, to Wright, and to James. And, in the conclusion, I discuss briefly some of Baldwin's later works as instances of the presumption of Baldwin's "maturity" and of his authority. I see Baldwin's problem of vocation as quintessentially American in certain crucial aspects, but unique, given the fact of race, in others. I see a rather complicated unity in the divergent traditions. In the epilogue, I offer some reflections of my own on the meaning of Baldwin's death.

This book combines a theoretical and explicatory approach and offers revisionary readings of Baldwin's early novels and essays. Readers will judge for themselves the ways in which my study is new; I consider it a rather protracted footnote to

the ongoing discussion of American and Afro-American literature. Whatever poststructuralist concerns implicitly emerge
are secondary; I have not attempted in any practical or system-
atic way to apply the work of any deconstructive or poststructuralist school. Nevertheless, readers will surely note in-
termittent glimmers of Harold Bloom's theory of the anxiety
of influence.

Bloom has written with such influential and overwhelming
intelligence on this topic that he is unavoidable. But even when
I use Bloom's terms—such as "revisionary" or "misread"—I
do not necessarily intend them in a specifically Bloomian context.[1] I appropriate his terms and use them in a general light
to suggest a diverse range of implicit and explicit, conscious
and unconscious, moments of intertextuality. I do not, for
example, read the relation between Baldwin and his precursors
in the strict "precursor" "ephebe" sense that Bloom's theory
and ideas presumably describe. Nor do I consider Baldwin's
"scene of instruction" in the manner Bloom designates; I consider Baldwin first in relation to three "strong" precursors,
one of whom he knew personally, Richard Wright, and two
whom he knew only from their writings, Harriet Beecher
Stowe and Henry James. My critical method, then, somewhat
mutes or compromises the overwhelming Oedipal prejudice
or privilege of Bloom's theory. Furthermore, since Bloom's
theory does not explicitly incorporate social or political matters, I found it of limited value when pondering the phenom-
enology of race in relation to the black writer's scene of either
writing or instruction. However, Bloom still remains attractive
to me because I share Vincent B. Leitch's observation that "in
opposition to deconstruction . . . [Bloom] aims to save the
human psyche, will, voice, and self from extinction by language, rhetoric, writing and the Other."[2]

In the case of Baldwin, a writer who tries relentlessly at the
outset of his career to avoid being looked upon as *merely* a

Negro; or, even, merely a Negro writer," a definitive and demonstrable element of race asserts itself in will, voice, and self. Race figures necessarily in my consideration of this writer's genesis. My reading of some of the hidden traces beneath the writer's prose of his ambivalence as writer and as black is partly what distinguishes this study from all previous work on Baldwin's literary career.

Horace Porter
Hanover, New Hampshire
July, 1988

ACKNOWLEDGMENTS

The support I have received from many individuals, to steal a phrase from James Baldwin, is "resolutely indefinable." However, without such support, this book would still be amid notes in a region of my mind. Cheers to you all—Carla Carr, Zachary E. Porter, James M. Cox, Louis A. Renza, William Ennis, Jerry Watts, Jeannette Hopkins, Peter J. Potter, Wilburn Williams, Jesse Young, Allen Guttmann, Robert G. O'Meally, Arnold Rampersad, Houston A. Baker, Jr., Donald Pease, Leo Marx, Todd Duncan, Blanche Gelfant, R. W. B. Lewis, Mike Thelwell, Joseph Prescott, Keith Walker, Alan Tractenberg, Elaine Jahner, Henry Louis Gates, Jr., Raymond L. Hall, Charles Feidelson, Jr., William Cook, Albert Rothenberg, Linda Morris, George R. Johnson, Jr., Deborah King, John Blassingame, John William Ward, Frank Moorer, Henry Terrie, David Porter, Abdul Kallon, Eliza Childs, Margaret Klumpp, Moira Palumbo, John Anderson, Joyce Kachergis, Lillie Mae Porter, Joseph Porter.

CHRONOLOGY

1924	Born on August 2 in Harlem Hospital, New York City.
1927	His mother, Emma Berdis Jones, marries David Baldwin.
1938–41	Preaches at Fireside Pentecostal Assembly.
1942	Graduates from DeWitt Clinton High School.
1942–43	Works on railroad in Belle Mead, New Jersey.
1943	Stepfather, David Baldwin, dies.
1944–45	Moves to Greenwich Village. Meets Richard Wright. Receives Eugene F. Saxton Memorial Trust Fellowship.
1948	Receives Rosenwald Fellowship. "The Harlem Ghetto" appears in *Commentary*. Sails for Paris.
1948–57	Lives in France and Switzerland.
1953	*Go Tell It on the Mountain*.
1954	Receives Guggenheim Fellowship.
1955	*Notes of a Native Son*.
1956	*Giovanni's Room*. Receives National Institute of Arts and Letters grant. Receives *Partisan Review* Fellowship.
1957	Returns to United States.
1959	Receives Ford Foundation grant-in-aid. Returns to Paris.

1960   Returns to United States.

1961   *Nobody Knows My Name: More Notes of a Native Son.*
        Leaves for Europe.

1962   *Another Country.*
        Leaves for Africa.

1963   *The Fire Next Time.*
        Receives George Polk Memorial Award.

1964   *Blues for Mister Charlie.*
        Nothing Personal.

1965   *Going to Meet the Man.*

1965–67   Lives in Europe and Turkey.

1968   *Tell Me How Long the Train's Been Gone.*
        The Amen Corner.

1971   *A Rap on Race: Margaret Mead and James Baldwin.*

1972   *No Name in the Street.*
        *One Day, When I Was Lost: A Scenario Based on Alex
        Haley's "The Autobiography of Malcolm X."*

1973   *A Dialogue: James Baldwin and Nikki Giovanni.*

1974   *If Beale Street Could Talk.*

1976   *The Devil Finds Work: An Essay.*
        Little Man, Little Man: A Story of Childhood.

1979   *Just Above My Head.*

1985   *Evidence of Things Not Seen.*
        The Price of the Ticket: Collected Nonfiction, 1948–1985.
        Jimmy's Blues.

1987   Dies on December 1, 1987, in St. Paul de Vence, France.
        Memorial service held at noon, December 8, at the
            Cathedral of St. John the Divine in New York City.
        Buried near the graves of Paul and Eslanda Goode
            Robeson at Ferncliff Cemetery, Ardsley, New York.

PROLOGUE
An Encounter at New Haven

When James Baldwin died on December 1, 1987, I had known the *writer* rather intimately for twenty-one years; but I did not know the man at all. For more than two decades, I had admired the writer at work, a genie in disguise, emerging full of wonder and surprise through the lines of his sparkling sentences.

I first heard of Baldwin in 1965 during Negro History Week when I was a freshman at William H. Spencer High School in Columbus, Georgia. My elementary and secondary education had been wholly segregated. From start to finish, it was about as black as it could be: classmates, teachers, principals, cooks, janitors. I had some outstanding teachers at Spencer High. But I did not read Baldwin because of my social situation. I read him in spite of it. None of his works was assigned in my high school courses. And coming from a working-class background, as I did, I knew no one who had even heard of *The Fire Next Time* or *Another Country,* Baldwin's best sellers during those years.

I stumbled across my first Baldwin volume quite by accident in the used-book section of a Salvation Army thrift shop. I was captivated by the title, blazing in bold red letters across a black background: *Nobody Knows My Name.* Was it luck or divine intervention? I still do not know. I would probably still be in Columbus, Georgia, today if I had not looked at the table of contents. "The Discovery of What It Means to Be an American," "A Fly in the Buttermilk," "The Black Boy Looks at the White Boy" inspired my deep curiosity. I knew immediately that I would get my money's worth—fifty cents—and something extra.

The essays were tough. I needed a dictionary from the first paragraph to the last. I highlighted things of note in red until the red in that slender volume almost overwhelmed the black. My vocabulary improved. But I quickly discovered that the dictionary alone was not always sufficient. I kept, for instance, puzzling over the word "conundrum," which Baldwin used frequently. In *my* dictionary "conundrum" was defined simply as a riddle. It clearly was more than that to Baldwin. The book became a minor encyclopedia for me. Baldwin referred to books, places, and ideas of which I was absolutely ignorant. He mentioned important individuals, especially writers, I literally did not know existed—Henry James, Bessie Smith, Norman Mailer, Albert Camus, Aimé Cesaire, Léopold Senghor, Jean-Paul Sartre, André Gide, Amos Tutuola.

I accepted all that Baldwin said, at least that which was comprehensible to me, without questions or qualifications. He wrote with Olympian assurance. Each sentence, even if it was a question, seemed unassailable: "But what is *Anna Karenina* describing if not the tragic fate of the isolated individual, at odds with her time and place?" Baldwin, with his daunting vocabulary, was beginning to work cosmopolitan magic on my inchoate adolescent sensibility.

Baldwin helped, figuratively, to arrange my flight from Columbus, Georgia, to Amherst College. Ironically, during the turbulent late 1960s and early 1970s, and during several long, snowy winters of discontent and nostalgia at Amherst, he even facilitated my spiritual journey back home. I read all of his books at Amherst. Thus, when I arrived at Yale for graduate work in American studies, it was hardly an accident that I decided, after several detours, to write my dissertation on his work.

During my years in New Haven, I thought I needed to interview Baldwin in order to complete my dissertation. Someone suggested that I contact his literary agent. I eventually tracked down his agent at that time, who was Jay Acton. So one day I found myself in Greenwich Village informing Mr. Acton that I was writing a dissertation on Baldwin and needed an interview. Mr. Acton was professional and gracious. He said he had told Baldwin about me; Baldwin had agreed we should meet. But he had not said, "Thursday at one p.m." The conversation with Acton was instructive in its own way. I found out, to my surprise, that Baldwin was not his most successful author. He was, if memory serves, third on the list. Helen Van Slyke, whom I still have not read, was Number One. I never interviewed Baldwin, then or later.

Several years passed. I accepted a teaching position at Wayne State University. While I was there, the Dean of Columbia College, Arnold Collery, a former professor at Amherst, called to invite me to a black-tie fund-raising dinner. Baldwin was scheduled to attend; the event was somehow related to his publisher, Dell Publishing. I rented a tuxedo and flew to New York. It was a big affair. And, while I am not given to keeping ethnic tabulations, I could not help noticing that only one other black person was in the room, an elderly gentleman who kept a polite distance. I seemed to be the youngest person there. I was beginning to feel like a displaced person, when a tall gentleman came over, looked down rather inquisitively, and said, "Hi, I'm Kurt Vonnegut." "I'm Horace Porter," I replied and smiled. He waited patiently and politely, as though expecting me to continue. I explained that I had flown in from Detroit to meet Baldwin. "He's not coming," he said. "I have never met him myself. I was looking forward to it."

Baldwin had apparently gotten the date confused and was in Washington. I felt personally insulted by his absence. After all, I had come all the way from Detroit to meet and hear

him. And three mayors of New York were in the room—John
Lindsay, Abraham Beame, and Edward Koch, the only one
not wearing a tuxedo. I tried to make the most of it. I chatted
with former Mayor Lindsay, who jokingly speculated that we
were probably the only two Yale men in the room. But even
Joseph Papp, donning a top hat and crooning "Brother, Can
You Spare a Dime?" did not console me. Where was James
Arthur Baldwin?

Later that year I moved from Wayne State to Dartmouth
College; I completed my dissertation. Several years later, when
Henry Louis Gates, a friend from the Yale days, came up from
New Haven to give a lecture, I learned that Baldwin would
give the Richard Wright Lecture at Yale. Professor Gates in-
vited me to attend. Was he certain Baldwin would show up?
Gates was encouraging and enthusiastic, but I was not entirely
convinced. A day before the scheduled event, I called to make
sure. Yes, Baldwin would be there.

I drove down to New Haven, listening to the news on the
radio. I thought about what I would say to Baldwin. I had
imagined this meeting for many years, and now at long last I
would really meet him. I arrived at the lecture hall a half hour
before Baldwin was scheduled to speak. The minutes ticked
by. Then James Baldwin, no longer a phantom, came in. He
was frail and intense. He had about him a celebrity's aura—
that heightened sense of self-consciousness, controlled self-
consciousness, that somehow served as a shield or screen
against our scrutiny. As he was introduced, the audience rose
to its feet applauding. Baldwin, smiling broadly and gra-
ciously, dug in his inner jacket for his notes. With a crumpled
piece of paper in hand, he held forth with remarkable eloquence for more than an hour. I noted, of course, that much
of what he said, while breathtakingly delivered, was essentially
a sustained variation on his essay about Wright, "Alas, Poor
Richard," published in the first book of his I had read, *Nobody*

Knows My Name. I had hoped for something different, something more. At the end, the audience rose again, applauding for a long time.

As the question-and-answer session was about to get started, a young black man, clearly not a Yale student, raised his hand and asked whether or not Baldwin would autograph a few books he had brought along. The master of ceremonies interceded. Baldwin would do so after the question-and-answer period. Others asked questions that are usually asked of famous writers. "What are you working on now, Mr. Baldwin?" He had just completed *Evidence of Things Not Seen,* his extended essay on the Atlanta child murders, and was now at work on a book about Dr. Martin Luther King, Medgar Evers, and Malcolm X. Then the young man raised his hand again. Baldwin tried to ignore him, but he insisted. He told Baldwin he liked some of his books. But, he asked, "how come you write all those gay books? I can't stand those." "Ha!" Baldwin replied and turned to the next questioner.

After the final question, Baldwin signed a few autographs. I waited patiently, walking along on the way to the reception as Baldwin chatted with a Yale student, black but fair-skinned, who told Baldwin he was frequently mistaken for an Algerian whenever he was in Paris. Professor Gates introduced me and told Baldwin I had written my dissertation on him. Baldwin shook my hand and stared through me penetratingly. The intensity of his gaze startled me. I felt like some nocturnal creature pierced by the bright beams of oncoming headlights. I told him, with pride, that I had read all of his books and all of the criticism of them. He said nothing. I broke the awkward moment of silence. "I'm from Columbus, Georgia," I said. "I've been there," he replied. And that was the beginning and the end of my personal encounter with James Baldwin.

I have thought seriously about it since. It was presumptuous, and rather adolescent, of me to believe that Baldwin would be warm to me. Many people wanted to talk to him. And all writers might well be wary of critics who write about them. Whatever the case, it was the only time we ever met. I retained my high respect for him and continued the relationship—that of the reader/critic—I had prior to our meeting. Even now, with his spirit out there among the stars, I commune with him. And I salute him.

INTRODUCTION
From Harlem to Paris: James Baldwin's Complex Fate

In Paris, I began to see the sky for what seemed to be the first time. It was borne in on me—and it did not make me feel melancholy—that this sky had been there before I was born and would be there when I was dead. And it was up to me, therefore, to make of my brief opportunity the most that could be made.

—James Baldwin, "The Discovery of What It Means
   to Be an American"

Perhaps somebody will one day discover in some hotel in Paris the four unpublished novels James Baldwin wrote before *Go Tell It on the Mountain*.[1] One cannot be sure what hidden treasures or literary evidence remain unseen; perhaps some will soon arrive from St. Paul de Vence. But whatever the volume or nature of any posthumous publication, James Baldwin's status as a major writer of the second half of the twentieth century appears reasonably assured. Future critics and biographers, considering Baldwin's complicated life and varied literary career, will qualify my judgment. But, whatever assessments scholars make, Baldwin has established a remarkable record. He wrote about race and sexuality for almost four decades. He published twenty-two books, among them six novels, a collection of short stories, two plays, several assortments of essays, a children's book, a movie scenario, and *Jimmy's Blues* (1985), a chapbook of poems.

I date and divide Baldwin's career into two phases, up to *The Fire Next Time* (1963) and after. Baldwin began during the late 1940s with book reviews and essays for *The New Leader, The Nation, Commentary,* and *Partisan Review.* His first significant essay was "The Harlem Ghetto" in *Commentary* (1948). "Everybody's Protest Novel" (1949) and "Many Thousands Gone" (1951), Baldwin's famous essays that take Stowe and Wright to task, were first published in *Partisan Review.* He wrote his first novel, *Go Tell It on the Mountain,* in 1953, after the essays began appearing.[2] "Everybody's Protest Novel" and "Many Thousand Gone," along with other essays, were collected and published in *Notes of a Native Son* in 1955. In the following year *Giovanni's Room* appeared. Then came, in swift succession, *Nobody Knows My Name* (1961), his second collection of essays; *Another Country* (1962), his controversial bestselling third novel; and the powerful essay *The Fire Next Time* (1963).[3] These works along with his play *Blues for Mister Charlie* (1964), which ran at the ANTA Theatre on Broadway, essentially constitute the dramatic end of the first phase.

Baldwin's writings after *The Fire Next Time* are all consciously political. He addressed complex social issues in his novels and in his essays. Leo Proudhammer, the protagonist of *Tell Me How Long the Train's Been Gone* (1968), like Baldwin, is a famous black artist (in his case an actor) who makes speeches for various Afro-American causes. In *No Name in the Street* (1972) Baldwin lashed out bitterly at an America whose moral bankruptcy was symbolized by the assassination of Dr. Martin Luther King. *If Beale Street Could Talk* (1974), while ostensibly a love story, dramatizes the travesty and inefficiency of the American criminal justice system. *The Devil Finds Work* (1976) is a scathing indictment of Hollywood's treatment of blacks in movies. In *Just Above My Head* (1979), his last novel, the narrator delivers frequent exhortations on diverse injustices in American life. *Evidence of Things Not Seen* (1985), a discussion of the Atlanta, Georgia, child murders, is an extended and fierce account of white hate. Baldwin also published *The Price of the Ticket: Collected Nonfiction 1948–1985*. In "Here Be Dragons," the volume's final essay, Baldwin discusses explicitly details of his homosexual life.

With publication of *The Fire Next Time* Baldwin became famous. It marked another crucial aspect not only of his literary career but also of his complex fate as an American. After its publication in 1963, a portrait of James Baldwin's face— dark, brooding, and intelligent—appeared on the cover of

Time magazine. The cover carried the caption "Birmingham and Beyond: The Negro's Push for Equality." The feature article begins with this description:

. . . James Baldwin, 38, . . . is nervous, slight, almost a fragile figure, filled with frets and fears. He is effeminate in manner, drinks considerably, smokes cigarettes in chains, and he often loses his audience with overblown arguments. Nevertheless, in the U.S. today there is not another writer—white or black—who expresses with such poignancy and abrasiveness the dark realities of the racial ferment in North and South.[4]

How he managed, in roughly fifteen years, to negotiate his way from the Harlem ghetto to Paris to the cover of *Time* and the center of national attention is an amazing story. Given his autobiographical essays, we know he was a self-made man in the most comprehensive sense of the phrase. His aggressive candor about his life has contributed to the public perception of him. We know, for example, that he was an accomplished writer, that he was black, that he was homosexual, and that he lived in, among other countries, France and Switzerland. He was the grandson of a slave and the stepson of a Southern-born Harlem preacher. He was, for two years during his adolescence, a preacher himself. Nevertheless, despite his extraordinary ethnic background, he asserts: "I left America because I doubted my ability to survive the fury of the color problem here. . . . I wanted to prevent myself from becoming merely a Negro; or, even, merely a Negro writer."[5]

Baldwin's preoccupation with racial categorization led to his criticisms of Harriet Beecher Stowe's *Uncle Tom's Cabin* and Richard Wright's *Native Son*. Yet in spite of that criticism, of Wright and of the protest tradition, and in spite of the precautionary literary measures he took to avoid becoming "*merely* a Negro; or, even, merely a Negro writer," his own complex fate as an American writer had already been sealed. The literary and social circumstances that motivated him to write, say, *The Fire Next Time* were, in a sense, predetermined. Baldwin acted out, in a complicated yet inexorable manner, a socioliterary role that black writers have been forced to play from slavery onward. Writing during the 1920s, W. E. B. Du Bois, in "The Social Origins of Negro Art," discussed this role of black writers as almost inevitable. He concluded: ". . . in most cases individual impulse was combined with a certain group compulsion, as we usually say, meaning that the wishes, thoughts, and experiences of thousands of individuals influence consciously and unconsciously the message of the one who speaks for all. That social compulsion in this case was built on the sorrow and the strain inherent in American slavery, on the difficulties that sprang from emancipation, on the feelings of revenge, despair, aspiration and hatred which arose as the Negro struggled and fought his way upward."[6]

Critics of Afro-American literature have, therefore, come routinely to consider Baldwin primarily a racial spokesman. His reputation is clouded by imprecise shibboleths. He is considered by many critics and readers to be an essayist who poses as a novelist. Other critics complain about the highly autobiographical content of his novels; they see Baldwin as a thinly disguised surrogate for his protagonists. Indeed, all of his writings, but especially his candid autobiographical essays are explained summarily as a relentless search for identity. Critics view this quest for identity almost exclusively in the context of large social questions or private personal matters, such as his homosexuality. None has attempted to look thoroughly at Baldwin's work as in any way affected by confluences and influences of American and Afro-American literature.

With one exception, the four book-length studies published to date concentrate on his "identity quest." Although Stanley Macebuh's *James Baldwin: A Critical Study* (1973), the first full-length critical work on Baldwin, provides remarkable readings of individual stories and novels, his work suffers from his inclination to view all of Baldwin's writings as a direct result of what he calls "theological terror," an "obsession with damnation."[7] In his own ambitious study, *James Baldwin* (1978), Louis H. Pratt examines Baldwin's stories, novels, plays, and essays.[8] But his chapter on Baldwin's essays devotes only two pages to his distinguished collection, *Notes of a Native Son*. Carolyn Sylvander's *James Baldwin* (1980), an excellent reader's guide to Baldwin's novels, plays, and short stories,[9] devotes only a brief chapter to Baldwin's voluminous nonfiction, and it is apparently not intended as an extended critical analysis of Baldwin's writings. Trudier Harris's *Black Women in the Fiction of James Baldwin* (1985) avoids the pitfalls of other studies.[10] By focusing on what appears to be a part of Baldwin's writing, on sexuality, gender, and race, she magnifies the whole. Thus, most approaches to Baldwin's writing have consistently been traditional.

Take the manner in which Pratt and Macebuh analyze Baldwin's first novel, *Go Tell It on the Mountain*. In *James Baldwin* Pratt describes *Go Tell It on the Mountain* as essentially "an exorcism, a purgation, a necessary constriction which leads, ultimately, to the unlimited expanses of self-identity. . . . *Go Tell It on the Mountain* stands as an honest, intensive, self-analysis, functioning simultaneously to illuminate self, society, and mankind as a whole."[11] Pratt provides a general synopsis of the more thorough commentary of Macebuh's *James Baldwin: A Critical Study*. Macebuh views John Grimes's quarrel with God and his stepfather, Gabriel, as the primary source of his anguish. *Go Tell It on the Mountain* is Baldwin's attempt to get "a sense of private theological danger" out of his system.[12] He sees both *Go Tell It on the Mountain* and *Giovanni's Room* as Baldwin's obsessive preoccupation with his own private world, and, thus, "an indispensable, if not mandatory, exercise in self-therapy."[13] Baldwin "had at first to rid himself of his psychic enslavement to the cosmology of damnation, and his

first two novels may legitimately, therefore, be seen as thera-
peutic rituals of exorcism in which the very act of confronta-
tion with theological dread bears within itself the potential
for destroying these fears."[14]

In "Fathers and Sons in James Baldwin's *Go Tell It on the
Mountain*," Michel Fabre writes that "the story reflects, barely
disguised, Baldwin's own life." He sees in it:

The same childhood: David Baldwin, a preacher, in actuality married
Emma Berdis Jones three years after James was born, but his stepfather preferred Sam (younger than James), his son by a previous
marriage, although his love was not returned. He detested James, on
whom devolved the care of the babies who were born after him. His
mother's right arm, James was also the ugly duckling of the tale,
"frog eyes," with his large eyes and overlarge mouth which his
schoolmates made fun of. He identified with Topsy, the gnome of
Uncle Tom's Cabin. . . . He was the youngster who climbed the hill
in Central Park and dreamed of grandeur.[15]

Numerous passages in *Go Tell It on the Mountain*, as Pratt,
Macebuh, and Fabre all maintain, do indeed readily lend themselves to autobiographical interpretation. One could persua-
sively read such passages as fictional counterparts of Baldwin's
comments in *Notes of a Native Son*, in *The Devil Finds Work*,
and in other autobiographical essays. But this direct referential
approach, in which the "facts" of John Grimes's life are cor-
rectly perceived as mirroring Baldwin's, amounts to only a
useful interpretative beginning, not a critical end. The point
of view from which one scrutinizes the facts of a writer's life
as writer is also crucial. Thus, the literal facts of Baldwin's
boyhood, so I believe, pale in significance beside the "secrets"
of his *literary* life embedded in the text of *Go Tell It on the
Mountain*.

Two passages readily illustrate this. In a rebellious moment
in *Go Tell It on the Mountain*, John imagines himself as a successful adult:

In this world John, who was, his father said, ugly, who was always the smallest boy in his class, and who had no friends, became immediately beautiful, tall, and popular. People fell all over themselves to meet John Grimes. He was a poet, or a college president, or a movie star; he drank expensive whiskey; and he smoked Lucky Strike cigarettes in the green package.

(Go Tell It on the Mountain, p. 19)

Earlier in the passage when the narrator refers to John's situation—"the darkness of his father's house . . . the darkness of his father's church"—or when John dreams of going "to the movies as often as he wished," one can believe such was, in literal fact, Baldwin's story. But if one takes the referential approach farther, one finds revelations about Baldwin's adolescent ambition in John's choice of idols, "a poet," "a college president," "a movie star," that suggest, prophetically, Baldwin's divided loyalties among the various roles he will find himself ambivalently assuming. The "poet," that is, pure artist, the "college president," that is, public figure, the "movie star," that is, celebrity, all eventually figure in Baldwin's complex fate.

But the deeper autobiographical strength found in *Go Tell It on the Mountain* surfaces in the signs of Baldwin's conscious and unconscious literary relationship to his literary forebears—Stowe, Wright, and James. The profound autobiography or self-writing that asserts itself like a disguised figure in the body of Baldwin's novel goes even beyond the portrait of a writer as a young man. Baldwin's, the writer's, life, the *literary* life, issues forth in an inexorably complex and ambivalent way, spelling out the splendid path of his contradictory literary career. The figure I see emerging is evident in a single passage—John's hilltop fantasy in Central Park. It seems prophetic in light of Baldwin's subsequent career.

John, at fourteen, is a brooding, precocious loner, simultaneously protected and isolated by his intelligence. His race, religion, and social status do not distinguish him among his peers, but his power of perception marks him. His sense of personal difference leads him to the hill in Central Park:

At a point that he knew by instinct and by the shape of the buildings surrounding the park, he struck out on a steep path overgrown with trees, and climbed a short distance until he reached the clearing that led to the hill. Before him, then, the slope stretched upward, and above it the brilliant sky, and beyond it, cloudy, and far away, he saw the skyline of New York. He did not know why, but there arose in him an exultation and a sense of power, and he ran up the hill like an engine, or a madman, willing to throw himself headlong into the city that glowed before him.

But when he reached the summit he paused; he stood on the crest of the hill, hands clasped beneath his chin, looking down. Then he, John, felt like a giant who might crumble this city with his anger; he felt like a tyrant who might crush this city beneath his heel; he felt like a long-awaited conqueror at whose feet flowers would be strewn, and before whom multitudes cried, Hosanna! He would be, of all, the mightiest, the most beloved, the Lord's anointed; and he would live in this shining city which his ancestors had seen with longing from far away. For it was his; the inhabitants of the city had told him it was his; he had but to run down, crying and they would take him to their hearts and show him wonders his eyes had never seen.

(*Go Tell It on the Mountain,* p. 33)

Critics, like Macebuh, Pratt, and Fabre, who read *Go Tell It on the Mountain* as essentially Baldwin's self-therapeutic attempt to exorcise his private theological demons and dreads, would probably interpret John's fantasy as clear textual evidence of their claim. John Grimes, like young James Baldwin, wishes to escape the dogmatically religious boundaries of his father's house. But much more is at work in John's fantasy. It represents Baldwin's unconscious distillation of his complex literary fate. The surge of power John feels, "the exultation," is fueled by his inchoate sense of the potentialities of his remarkable intelligence. Thus, he imagines another world of promise and rich possibility—a world elsewhere. But even though he sees the lights of downtown Manhattan glowing before him, that world remains as charmingly elusive and distant as London to Dick Whittington. Furthermore, Baldwin's mixing of John's imaginative construction with concrete reality, his bringing together of the public and private in this scene, is of crucial significance. When John Grimes stares at the shining city downtown, Baldwin's literary future is revealed as though encapsulated in a fortune teller's crystal ball.

Since John Grimes knows the point in Central Park "by instinct" and since he "struck out" for it, Baldwin suggests that his is a recurrent fantasy that he is driven to act out. "He did not know why, but there arose in him an exultation and a sense of power, and he ran up the hill like an engine, or a madman." The setting, Central Park, is a noted public space in America's largest and most influential city. Thus, John's fantasy also betrays genuine ambition and a personality marked by the need of consummate self-expression. John's adolescent self gives way to a raging spirit within him, which the narrator likens to that of a "madman," but the metaphorical resonance of the passage does not suggest madness so much as profoundly troubling ambivalence. The fantasy is, of course, symptomatic of John Grimes's struggle with the cosmology of his father's house, but it also represents Baldwin's early meditation on his literary fate. The immediate scene is superimposed on a more significant aspect almost hidden in John's avenging imagination, the portrait of an ambitious young artist with a confident and raging will to public expression and power. The temptations John sees tantalizingly before him are implicitly literary in nature. The temptations concern questions and choices inextricably bound to his becoming and being a black American writer.

John Grimes pauses at the summit because the future he perceives through the light of his precocious clairvoyance combines splendor with terror. The glowing lights symbolize Manhattan's electric glory and future promise as well as its ruthless, anthropomorphic indifference. John's feelings are analogous to young Baldwin's own. He in turn feels, say, like Richard Wright, the current black literary "giant" or "tyrant" who by creating *Native Son* and Bigger Thomas "might crumble this city with his anger . . . who might crush this city beneath his heel." Or he would become, like his idol, Henry James, "the mightiest." Or perhaps, like Stowe, he would write in a divinely inspired manner and become "the Lord's anointed." John's fantasy represents Baldwin's inspired vision of his literary future. It is defined by a combination of ambivalent impulses—anger, faith, and love—as well as a preoccupation with public status, fame, and power.

Since *Go Tell It on the Mountain* ends before John chooses a profession, his future must remain a matter of conjecture. But Baldwin the writer does achieve fame and recognition similar to what John imagines in his fantasy. It forecasts his willingness to occupy such a demanding socioliterary position in society.

I "A RAGE IN THE BLOOD"
The Significance of "Notes of a Native Son"

Negroes are Americans, and their destiny is the country's destiny. They have no other experience besides their experience on this continent and it is an experience which cannot be rejected, which yet remains to be embraced. If, as I believe, no American Negro exists who does not have his private Bigger Thomas living in the skull, then what most significantly fails to be illuminated here is the paradoxical adjustment which is perpetually made, the Negro being compelled to accept the fact that this dark and dangerous and unloved stranger is part of himself forever. Only this recognition sets him in any wise free.

—James Baldwin, "Many Thousands Gone"

Baldwin's title essay in *Notes of a Native Son* is an autobiographical tour de force.[1] Its title, while seeming to exploit or appropriate in an obvious way the title of Richard Wright's *Native Son* and Henry James's *Notes of a Son and Brother*, is not as simple as that.[2] First, "notes" suggests something provisional, temporary, or inconclusive; in that light, it is synonymous with "outline." But "notes" tells us something more meaningful in what it suggests about the essay's symbolic significance for the writer's literary career. In that context the word can be read as "prologue." Baldwin had published only one book before *Notes of a Native Son*. He had just turned thirty. *Notes of a Native Son* constitutes Baldwin's first decisive efforts as a professional writer. The individual essays had actually appeared in various magazines before the publication, in 1953, of his first novel, *Go Tell It on the Mountain*. Essays like "The Harlem Ghetto," "Everybody's Protest Novel," and "Many Thousands Gone" were quite literally his debut as a writer. He wrote them when he was in his twenties. So the word "notes" suggests a kind of prelude—the dramatic opening chords proclaiming a literary event of public note.

"Notes of a Native Son" also suggests the idea of family. Baldwin's status as "son" will be in the foreground. But even if we are unfamiliar with the details of his life—the fact, for instance, that he had been a child evangelist—the essay promptly tells us that through the intimation of the biblical parable of the prodigal son. Thus, Baldwin becomes considerably more than the stepson of a Negro minister in the Harlem ghetto. He is a son of God and a citizen of the world. The family in question is the human family with its multifarious range of terrors and wonders.

Baldwin begins his essay on a universal note, connecting his life and his family's life to all mankind. A man dies; a child is born. He tells us in his opening sentences: "On the 29th of July, in 1943, my father died. On the same day, a few hours later his last child was born." The essay is divided into three sections, paralleling the three sections—"Fear," "Flight," and "Fate"—of Wright's *Native Son*. Baldwin devotes the first to a description and candid examination of what he calls "the intolerable bitterness of spirit" in which his father (actually his stepfather) lived and died. He shows dramatically how his father's bitterness and fanatical asceticism deeply affected the lives of his nine children; so much, in fact, that they resent his very presence. And their father in turn believes, Baldwin says, that his children "had betrayed him by . . . reaching towards the world which had despised him." Baldwin is chief among the traitors. He is utterly contemptuous of his father's world view. His father warns him of the poisonous effects of white prejudice and hatred. He tells his son that even those white classmates he considers his best friends are not to be trusted. Baldwin rejects this warning. This, among other disagreements, compels him to leave his father's house, and after he has graduated from high school, he leaves Harlem for Trenton, New Jersey, to take a job in a defense plant. His co-workers are mostly black and white Southerners. He is rudely awakened by their hostile responses to him. He is fired after a while, and on his last night in Trenton, when he is refused service at a fashionable restaurant, he explodes in an unexpected fit of murderous rage.

In the second section of the essay, Baldwin, the prodigal son, returns home. He knows his father is dying and that his mother is about to give birth to another child. Baldwin's description of Harlem and its somber wartime mood leads to the essay's final section, a poignant recapitulation, complete with cinematic effects, of his father's funeral. Through a stunning series of deftly arranged flashbacks, we witness Baldwin responding to his father, first as an angry son approaching manhood, then as a rebellious adolescent, and finally as a small boy. Baldwin carefully prepares the reader for his revelations. His central theme is the complex legacy his father left him. The son—reflective and troubled—must ponder perpetually the self-destructive black rage and bitterness fueled in his father and then in himself by the prejudice of white Americans. Baldwin examines the capricious nature of the black rage he feels, an anger simultaneously personal and collective. His experience is, of course, specific but it is hardly unique; every black American is somehow victimized by racial prejudice. Thus, Baldwin's essay, even in the most literal way, reminds one of Wright's *Native Son*.

This link is established in the essay's first section, in which Baldwin is a victim of overt racial discrimination. Using a telling form of symbolic suggestion, he recounts the story of that last night in Trenton. He and a white friend go out on the town and see a movie titled *This Land Is Mine*. That ironical and suggestive title is highlighted when the reader discovers that the diner they go to after the movie is called the American Diner. Baldwin asks for a hamburger and a cup of coffee, and is rebuffed by the counterman. He is told, "'We don't serve Negroes here.'" After a brief, sharp reply, Baldwin and his white friend walk out into the street: "People were moving in every direction but it seemed to me, in that instant, that all of the people I could see, and many more than that, were moving toward me, against me, and that everyone was white. . . . I wanted to do something to crush these white faces which were crushing me." As in a trance, Baldwin then comes

to the door of an "enormous, glittering, and fashionable restaurant," where, he knows, "not even the intercession of the
virgin" will allow him to be served. He enters the restaurant,
nevertheless, sits at a table for two, and waits. When the
young white waitress, with "great, astounded, frightened eyes,"
comes over and predictably announces, "'We don't serve
Negroes here,'" Baldwin loses control. He throws a water mug
at her with all his strength. It misses and shatters against the
mirror behind the bar. Suddenly he comes to his senses: "I
saw, for the first time, the restaurant, the people with their
mouths open, already as it seemed to me, rising as one man.
. . . I rose and began running for the door." Baldwin's friend
misdirects his pursuers and the police, and after Baldwin is
alone and safe, he ponders the event over and over and arrives
at two shocking and alarming conclusions: "I could not get
over two facts, both equally difficult for the imagination to
grasp, and one was that I could have been murdered. But the
other was that I had been ready to commit murder. I saw . . .
that my life, my *real* life, was in danger, and not from anything
other people might do but from the hatred I carried in my
own heart." The murderous rage Baldwin feels is clearly reminiscent of Bigger Thomas's blind hatred and anger. But Baldwin hopes the love he has in his heart will serve as an antidote,
mitigating the effects of his poisonous, self-destructive bitterness. The essential emotional drama of the essay arises from
his dilemma: How can a native son whose democratic American dreams must seemingly be perpetually deferred strike the
necessary balance between love and hate? All of his work thereafter would elaborate that theme.

In the second section, when Baldwin visits his father in the
hospital, the sight of his father as he lies dying awakens Baldwin's compassion: "The great, gleaming apparatus which fed
him and would have compelled him to be still even if he had
been able to move brought to mind, not beneficence, but tor-

ture; the tubes entering his arm made me think of pictures I had seen when a child of Gulliver, tied down by the pygmies on that island."

In the final section Baldwin explores the significance of his father's life and death. And, through that process, he discovers something about the nature of the hatred and bitterness he carries in his own heart. He reminds the reader that the day of his father's funeral had also been his own nineteenth birthday. He had spent most of the day downtown at the apartment of a girl he knew. They celebrated by drinking and tried to focus on Baldwin's birthday rather than on the funeral that night. This particular detail is telling in a special way. The birthday celebration, such as it was, was a pretext for Baldwin's temporary and what became, eventually, in a special way, a permanent departure from his father's house and his father's world. Thus, even on the day of his father's funeral, Baldwin appears to be headed in the direction of another country, another culture.

Baldwin's father saw downtown Manhattan as a city of sin and corruption rivaled only by Sodom and Gomorrah. Baldwin is attempting to escape the overwhelming power of his religious tradition, and his success in escaping will remain in question. Even on the most superficial level, he worries about the appropriateness of his behavior. A "nagging problem" has oppressed him "all day long"—the fact that he has nothing black to wear to the funeral. Baldwin understands that a funeral ritual is a necessary and proper ending in human affairs. As he says, "Every man in the chapel hoped that when his hour came he, too, would be eulogized, which is to say forgiven, and that all of his lapses, greeds, errors, and strayings from the truth would be invested with coherence and looked upon with charity." Baldwin certainly knows, even at nineteen, that his religious convictions are not universally shared downtown. But he will share the cultural assumptions of the mourners who will come. The girl who is drinking and celebrating his birthday with him finds him a black shirt for the occasion, and, as Baldwin remembers, "dressed in the darkest pants and jacket I owned, and slightly drunk, I made my way to my father's funeral."

"It seemed to me, of course, that it was a very long funeral," Baldwin writes. "But it was, if anything, a rather shorter funeral than most, nor, since there were no overwhelming, uncontrollable expressions of grief, could it be called—if I dare to use the word—successful." Baldwin reaches a kind of autobiographical stasis at the funeral. He recovers a memory that heightens the intensity and sharpens the tone of the moment. We see and hear the young writer moving slightly away from his theme like an accomplished musician guided by a magical spell of improvisation. "While the preacher talked . . . my mind was busily breaking out with a rash of disconnected impressions. Snatches of popular songs, indecent jokes, bits of books I had read, movie sequences, faces, voices, political issues—I thought I was going mad." Even as Baldwin breaks away from his straightforward description of the funeral and describes his own intense interiority, even as he concentrates on what appears to be a predictable emotional reaction of loss and incipient grief occasioned by his father's death, the real focus is on the young writer himself. The things that are rising up, perhaps out of the deep blue of repressed memory, are not, at first, specific, or at least he does not report them as such. They are essentially abstract agents of narrative association— "snatches of popular songs," "bits of books," "movie sequences." What one might call the writer's characteristic disposition toward extraordinary mental association surges up and is played upon. Thus, we arrive at the moment where Baldwin, like Proust's Marcel, relives his own past:

Then someone began singing one of my father's favorite songs and, abruptly, I was with him, sitting on his knee, in the hot, enormous

crowded church which was the first church we attended. It was the
Abyssinian Baptist Church on 138th Street. . . . With this image, a
host of others came. I had forgotten, in the rage of my growing up,
how proud my father had been of me when I was little. Apparently,
I had had a voice and my father had liked to show me off before the
members of the church. I had forgotten what he looked like when
he was pleased but now I remembered that he had always been
grinning with pleasure when my solos ended. I even remembered
certain expressions on his face when he teased my mother. . . . I
remembered being taken for a haircut and scraping my knee on the
footrest of the barber's chair and I remembered my father's face as
he soothed my crying and applied the stinging iodine.

("Notes of a Native Son," p. 107)

Some readers may have experienced an analogous, vicarious,
moment. Pulled into the swirling vortex of the essay's central
theme, the legacy of the death of the father, the reader connects Baldwin's memory to his or her own sense, actual or
potential, of loss and grief. The song each reader hears in his
or her mind's ear is not the song Baldwin hears, but a song
of personal identification and a note of counterpoint. Baldwin
plays a universal note and touches a familiar nerve. Even more
significant is the precise nature of the memory. Baldwin cap-
tures the "forgotten" moments of the past as they surface on
the wave of memory induced by the sound of one of his father's "favorite songs." He is recalled, through song, to his
original relationship to his father. Now there is no cacophon-
ous collage of "popular songs," "bits of books," and "movie
sequences," but rather memories that are specific and somewhat separate. With each repetition, indeed each playing of
the word "remembered," a new scene unfolds. Now we see
the little boy on his father's knee, now the smiling face of the
proud father at the end of his son's solo, now we see the little
son summoning forth his father's consoling hand.

Baldwin's emphasis on music is telling, whether it is his
unexpected memory of popular songs, his recalling of the sing-

ing of his father's favorite songs, or the shocking recognition and remembrance of his own youthful church solos; all of the music is connected to the theme of the dead father. The theme of music looms large in the essay because "Notes of a Native Son" is, essentially, the solo Baldwin could not sing for his father at his father's final hour. It is the best that Baldwin can do, now that his father is dead and, no matter the intensity and power of memory, irrecoverable. And the solo is part and parcel of the moving picture we see of Baldwin's father. Viewed from one angle, his father is a brutal and bitter man; from another he is the victim, like many anonymous thousands, of racial prejudice and discrimination; from yet another he is a religious fanatic with a tempestuous personality; and finally, he is the smiling, proud, protective, and loving father of Baldwin's youth.

The memorable passage reflects the essay's multifaceted design. On a superficial, as well as a more profound, level, "Notes of a Native Son" is a classic instance of protest. Its message is clear. It is the story of a son who tries relentlessly to escape the crippling environment of his father's house. Along the way, the religious father views the son as a prodigal ingrate. But the willful son's extraordinary insistence upon his own vision of American life, his choice of writing over preaching, eventually provides the means by which he moves beyond the circumscribed limits of his father's house. Using his narrative resourcefulness, Baldwin rescues his essay from the banality of a predictable, if justifiable, Afro-American cry of racial prejudice and discrimination to a universal story of potential liberation of the self.

Baldwin's narrative ingenuity is complicated by his use of devices that are suggestive of certain cinematic techniques—including the use of voice-overs, collages, and flashbacks spliced seamlessly into the ongoing autobiographical narrative. Take, for example, the recurrent theme of the death of the father. When Baldwin brings the reader out of the flashback that leads the essay back to sweet memories of his childhood, he rolls his narrative abruptly away from the "forgotten " but now "remembered" world of his childhood and adolescence back into the enormous present of the church and the ongoing funeral. We see him staring at his father's open casket as the mourners, including his aunt and younger brothers and sisters, are led "one by one" to the bier. Then it is Baldwin's momentous turn:

One of the deacons led me up and I looked on my father's face. I cannot say that it looked like him at all. His blackness had been equivocated by powder and there was no suggestion in that casket of what his power had or could have been. He was simply an old man dead, and it was hard to believe that he had ever given anyone either joy or pain. Yet, his life filled that room. Further up the avenue his wife was holding his newborn child. Life and death so close together, and love and hatred, and right and wrong, said something to me which I did not want to hear concerning man, concerning the life of man.

("Notes of a Native Son," p. 109)

The technique appropriated from the cinema is tried and true. He shows the audience a close-up of a dead man's face and body. At first glance it appears to be a cheap shot, pandering, via sensationalism and sentimentality, to stock emotions. But Baldwin presents emotions far more complicated. He focuses on the reaction of the mourner. We are reminded that the son is seeing his father for the last time. And the son observes his father's face "equivocated by powder." It is as though the undertaker, realizing some hidden aspect of personality, had tried to protect the dead man's face from the cold scrutiny of the living. But Baldwin's use of "equivocate" suggests that what the undertaker had intended to be a charitable, face-saving device has failed. Baldwin recognizes the hopeless ethnic phenomenon of applying white powder to black skin. The white powder, designed to save the face by softening its features and presumably setting them free, actually imprisons. It reminds the son of his father's self-hatred and bitterness and the white hatred that had helped to destroy him.

By playing upon this moment of finality, Baldwin reminds us of the universal nature of the scene. Standing before his father's casket, he becomes the disembodied and timeless voice of mankind by way of his evocative rhetoric about the implacable forces and facts of the human condition. His is a choruslike and representative voice, reminding us of the eternal recurrence of "life and death," "love and hatred," "right and wrong."

After the funeral, Baldwin goes back downtown to continue celebrating his birthday, and, while his father lies in state in the undertaker's chapel, a riot breaks out in Harlem. Baldwin connects his father's funeral to the chaos and violence in the Harlem streets and exploits the riot's symbolic significance: "As we drove him to the graveyard, the spoils of injustice, anarchy, discontent, and hatred were all around us. It seemed to me that God himself had devised, to mark my father's end, the most sustained and brutally dissonant of codas." By setting his father's death and funeral in the context of a race riot, he suggests that his father's death is a matter of far-reaching public, not only private, significance. But beyond that, and moving directly from one of the connotations of "notes" in his title, he uses "coda," which signifies the formal ending of a musical composition. But the harmonious closure that characterizes a coda is nonexistent. The symbolic notes surrounding his father's death are troubling and discordant. Baldwin writes with poignancy about the death and funeral of his father eleven years after the fact in order to understand his own. Baldwin, just shy of thirty, is still, in effect, starting out as a writer. Thus, in crucial ways, "Notes of a Native Son" can be read as an autobiographical position paper. As we shall see, it is an implicit extension of his earlier comments in "Everybody's Protest Novel" and "Many Thousands Gone."

In the essays in *Notes of a Native Son*, Baldwin is attempting to create order out of the disorder of his own life. Indeed "Everybody's Protest Novel" and "Many Thousands Gone," though ostensibly literary criticism, are as vital and profoundly autobiographical as "Notes of a Native Son." Writing, for Baldwin, is a matter of life and death. And that essential exercise in personal and vocational clarification requires an extended examination of self, society, and history. It requires an analysis of how the three simultaneously conspire against and corroborate one's fate. In this context, the death of Baldwin's father cries out for interpretation. Thus, when the son, the aspiring writer, takes his last look at his father's face, he yearns for definitive answers. But the only authoritative answer his father, like any dead father, can give is symbolic. On one level the son is finally free. He is released from his father's house, if not entirely from his influence, in order to cultivate his own garden. Baldwin ponders the future as his father is driven "through a wilderness of smashed plate glass" to the graveyard. Focusing on the street, Baldwin uses another device appropriated from cinematic narration, this time, cinema verité. The camera, which is the "I" of Baldwin, the participant observer, simply follows the riotous *tableau vivant* as it unfolds on the Harlem street:

. . . bars, stores, pawn shops, restaurants, even little luncheonettes had been smashed open and entered and looted. . . . The shelves really looked as though a bomb had struck them. Cans of beans and soup and dog food, along with toilet paper, corn flakes, sardines and milk tumbled every which way, and abandoned cash registers, cases of beer leaned crazily out of the splintered windows and were strewn along the avenues. Sheets, blankets, and clothing of every description formed a kind of path, as though people had dropped them while running. I truly had not realized that Harlem *had* so many stores until I saw them all smashed open.

("Notes of a Native Son," p. iii)

Although, at the essay's beginning, Baldwin has described the riot as "the most sustained and brutally dissonant of codas," arranged by God to signal his father's end, he discovers, as his father is being driven to the graveyard, that the cacophony of the streets is also unmistakably his own. It reminds him of the rage and bitterness within him that may erupt suddenly and uncontrollably. The riot is also Harlem's collective black rage monstrously personified. On a more profound and perhaps even prophetic level, the riot is an intimation of what is in store for America. This scene anticipates the precautionary exhortations of *The Fire Next Time,* which would be written just before another time of turmoil and death.

The description of the riot, coming as it does near the essay's end, affords a narrative opportunity of dramatic poetic closure. Orchestrating a form of counterpoint in which the narrator observes Harlem disintegrating, the writer makes us privy to his interior monologue as he struggles to salvage personal and symbolic meaning out of the wreckage around him. We are shown the final flashback, which is not so much a scene in the sense of an actual place or incident as it is a private region in Baldwin's mind. He recalls his father's favorite biblical text, what Baldwin calls "the golden text":

And if it seem evil unto you to serve the Lord, choose you this day whom you will serve; whether the gods which your fathers served that were on the other side of the flood, or the gods of the Amorites, in whose land ye dwell: but as for me and my house, we will serve the Lord.

("Notes of a Native Son," p. 113)

By remembering his father's "golden text," characterized by an either-or scenario, Baldwin underscores the fact that he will be forced to reflect upon his failure to follow in his father's footsteps and "serve the Lord." A consideration of his father's text takes him back to his own days of adolescent evangelical fervor, back to that momentous occasion when his father rebuked him: "You'd rather write than preach, wouldn't you?"

The young evangelist's answer that fateful Sunday afternoon was "Yes." But his was hardly a simple answer. By replying "Yes," he was saying "No" to his father's whole way of life.

The rage Baldwin felt when he was nineteen, the riot he witnessed, and the memories he recalled during his father's funeral would only later achieve their full significance. Thus, reflecting on his father's death as the hearse rolls through the "wilderness of smashed plate glass," Baldwin concludes, "All of my father's texts and songs, which I had decided were meaningless, were arranged before me at his death like empty bottles, waiting to hold the meaning which life would give them for me. This was his legacy: nothing is ever escaped." Baldwin's use of the phrases "texts and songs . . . arranged . . . like empty bottles," though oddly mixed, derives crucial significance through the agency of subconscious or subliminal metaphorical suggestion. The songs and texts are "arranged." And since they are like "empty bottles," they can be viewed as a form of musical notation to be played out or played upon by the son. Since the "arranged" composition is inescapable, the son can, of course, willfully misread the composition or he can improvise. But the composition will always remain the point of departure. And the degree to which the son succeeds or fails will, at least in part, depend on his ability to translate or transpose the composition and arrangement of the songs and texts for his own purposes. Moreover, the empty bottles Baldwin refers to as his father's "legacy" might be compared to a series of precious burial urns. Viewed in this light, the bottles become the final resting place of his dead father's spirit. And Baldwin's memory becomes a mantel on which the bottles will remain forever "arranged." Of course, from time to time, the "golden text" will surface unexpectedly with genielike fidelity: "Now the whole thing came back to me as though my father and I were on our way to Sunday school." Baldwin's memory of and response to his father's golden text underscores

Kafka's observation that all profound writing is a kind of prayer. Baldwin's prayer simultaneously seeks the wisdom of his dead father and that of the living God the Father to whom his dead father was faithful to the end.

During this period of his life, Baldwin is compelled to interpret the meaning of his father's death in order to get on with his own life. He addressed this question in an introduction, written in 1984, to a new edition of *Notes of a Native Son*. Baldwin defines the words "inheritance" and "birthright"; he views inheritance as "particular, specifically limited and limiting." One's "birthright" is another matter; it connects him "to all that lives, and to everyone, forever." Calling the "conundrum of color" the inheritance of all Americans and asserting that "one cannot claim the birthright without accepting the inheritance," Baldwin concludes:

I was trying to locate myself within a specific inheritance, precisely, to claim the birthright from which the inheritance had so brutally and specifically excluded me. It is not pleasant to be forced to recognize, more than thirty years later, that neither this dynamic nor this necessity has changed.

(*"Notes of a Native Son,"* p. xii)

Baldwin's rather intense concern with his birthright drives him to distill that which is universal out of the "limited and limiting" disorder of the particular in "Notes of a Native Son." "The dead man mattered, the new life mattered; blackness and whiteness did not matter; to believe that they did was to acquiesce in one's own destruction."

"Notes of a Native Son" is a brilliant example of Baldwin's efforts to arrive at or claim his birthright by focusing on his inheritance. Yet his separation of "inheritance" from "birthright" is an academic dichotomy. What, we might be inclined to ask, would the term birthright mean to him if American life were not racially rigged? The idealistic democratic rhetoric describing certain "inalienable" rights—life, liberty, and the pursuit of happiness—is comprehensive. Perhaps Baldwin has in mind a subtle spiritual realization. Whatever the case, Baldwin dramatizes in "Notes of a Native Son" how inheritance can cripple and eventually destroy, particularly if that inheritance is defined by bitterness and rage. Such was the nature of his father's legacy. At the essay's end, we hear a note of compromise and deference in Baldwin's voice: "Now that my father was irrecoverable, I wished that he had been beside me so that I could have searched his face for the answers which only the future would give me now."

Baldwin's tone is also apprehensive. During that year in Trenton, when he was so often rebuffed, he felt as though he had contracted a "chronic disease":

. . . the unfailing symptom of which is a kind of blind fever, a pounding in the skull and fire in the bowels. Once this disease is contracted, one can never really be carefree again, for the fever, without an instant's warning can recur at any moment. . . . There is not a Negro alive who does not have this rage in his blood—one has the choice, merely, of living with it consciously or surrendering to it. As for me, this fever has recurred in me, and does, and will until the day I die.

("Notes of a Native Son," p. 94)

This is indicative of Baldwin's recognition of the rage in his own heart, a rage symbolized by the riot-torn streets of Harlem. Thus, Baldwin takes care to push the essay in the direction of the future. His father's death was certainly momentous, but, as he reminds us at the essay's end, the birth of his baby sister was also a significant event. "The new life mattered." He suggests that each time a child is born, regardless of the parents or life circumstances, the extraordinary potentiality of the human race is born again.

Baldwin's struggle to clarify the significance of his father's life and death in the context of his own is deeply related to his literary ambition. After he is released from the tyranny of his father's house, he discovers two literary parents—Harriet Beecher Stowe and Richard Wright—standing in his path.

II "THIS WEB OF LUST AND FURY"
Harriet Beecher Stowe, James Baldwin's Nineteenth-Century White Mother

I had read *Uncle Tom's Cabin* compulsively, the book in one hand, the newest baby on my hipbone. I was trying to find out something, sensing something in the book of immense import for me: which, however, I knew I did not really understand.

My mother got scared. She hid the book. The last time she hid it, she hid it on the highest shelf above the bathtub. I was somewhere around seven or eight. God knows how I did it, but I somehow climbed up and dragged the book down. Then, my mother, as she herself puts it, "didn't hide it anymore," and, indeed, from that moment, though in fear and trembling, began to let me go.

—James Baldwin, *The Devil Finds Work*

In "Everybody's Protest Novel," the opening essay in *Notes of a Native Son,* written in 1949 when James Baldwin was twenty-four, we see what Irving Howe appropriately describes as "gestures of repudiation, glimmers of intention."[1] Critics have failed to discuss the essay beyond what is usually considered Baldwin's harsh and opportunistic assessment of Harriet Beecher Stowe and of Richard Wright.[2] But it should be noted and counted singularly to Baldwin's credit that he does choose to discuss Stowe's *Uncle Tom's Cabin.* His choice (in the context of recent criticism about the novel) reveals his critical precociousness. He perceives and acknowledges, at twenty-four, the novel's uncanny socioliterary power. Although he attacks it scathingly, he spells out his position nearly forty years before professional literary critics would make a concerted rediscovery of what is now considered its inestimable literary value. Nor is his critique of the novel a literary fluke. It provides extraordinary evidence that this then unknown young black writer, writing with Jamesian syntax, already had a special and engaging angle of vision on American literary culture and social life.

The essay reveals, if inadvertently, a paradigmatic instance, articulately and contradictorily rendered, of a black writer starting out in America. His subject, the ironic legacy and horrible consequences of slavery, has already been given to him—even as he willfully and ambivalently turns away from it. Eschewing the artistic limitations of the protest tradition,

he states, "What is today parroted as his [the writer's] Responsibility—which seems to mean that he must make formal
declaration that he is involved in, and affected by, the lives of
other people and to say something improving about this somewhat self-evident fact—is, when he believes it, his corruption
and our loss."[3] But other aspects of the essay take us considerably beyond its implicit characterization of Baldwin's genesis
as a writer. He provides a capsule summary of what will become the central theme in his writings and life. While ostensibly considering the limitations of the protest novel in general
and the specific artistic failure of *Uncle Tom's Cabin* in particular, Baldwin proffers his criticism of white America's guilt-
ridden vision of black humanity.

Thus, a crucial aspect of Baldwin's essay concerns white
America's denial of—in American literature no less than in American life—the complexity of black humanity. In that light, he
discusses *Uncle Tom's Cabin* as characteristic documentation of
the self-destructive American vision that is as much a part of
the American present as of the American past. Speaking of
Stowe's novel, he asks, ". . . why are we bound still within the
same constriction? How is it that we are so loath to make a
further journey than that made by Mrs. Stowe, to discover and
reveal something a little closer to the truth?" "Everybody's
Protest Novel" displays what will emerge as Baldwin's preoccupation with the mythic, categorical perception and portrayal
of blacks. He views Stowe's depiction of blacks as stereotypical,
perniciously sentimental, and also violent:

Uncle Tom's Cabin is a very bad novel, having, in its self-righteous,
virtuous sentimentality, much in common with *Little Women*. Sentimentality, the ostentatious parading of excessive and spurious emo-
tion, is the mark of dishonesty, the inability to feel; the wet eyes
of the sentimentalist betray his aversion to experience, his fear of
life, his arid heart; and it is always, therefore, the signal of secret
and violent inhumanity, the mask of cruelty. *Uncle Tom's Cabin*

—like its multitudinous, hard-boiled descendants—is a catalogue of violence.

("Everybody's Protest Novel," p. 14)

Baldwin's tone is captious and polemical when he asserts that Stowe's sentimentality "is the mark of dishonesty, the inability to feel . . . the signal of secret and violent inhumanity." Baldwin maintains that protest novels, like *Uncle Tom's Cabin,* instead of advancing the cause of black Americans actually strengthen the common myths, stereotypes, and prejudices about them. He argues that Stowe places a higher premium on sensationalism than on revelation. Thus, hard truths about the experience of the slaves and their masters are cruelly and superficially masked by what Baldwin calls Stowe's "catalogue of violence," her descriptions of "unmotivated and senseless" brutality. He charges that she leaves the only important question "unanswered and unnoticed"—she fails to show "what moved her people to such deeds." It would appear as though Baldwin's primary criticism of *Uncle Tom's Cabin* concerns aesthetic matter. He accuses Stowe of a failure of artistic imagination and execution. But, given the novel's extraordinary popularity, he certainly had the social consequences of her artistic failure in mind. Despite the protest novel's "avowed aim . . . to bring greater freedom to the oppressed," Baldwin views it as "a mirror of our confusion, dishonesty, panic." He writes, "Whatever unsettling questions are raised are evanescent, titillating, remote, for this has nothing to do with us, it is safely ensconced in the social arena, where indeed, it has nothing to do with anyone, so that finally we receive a very definite thrill of virtue from the fact that we are reading such a book at all." Referring to *Gentleman's Agreement* and *The Postman Always Rings Twice* as exemplary of the same myths and fallacies found in Stowe's novel, Baldwin concludes, "in *Uncle Tom's Cabin* we may find a foreshadowing of both: the formula created by the necessity to find a lie more palatable than the truth has been handed down and memorized and persists yet with a terrible power."

As Baldwin views it, Stowe's self-righteous, purposeful desire merely to "prove that slavery was wrong" leads to an artistic failure. Thus, he considers her portrayal of her black characters as stereotypical. He refers to her "lively procession" of field hands and house niggers as "stock lovable figures." He ridicules the three most important black characters in the novel—Uncle Tom and George and Eliza Harris. He describes Uncle Tom as a stereotype: "jet-black, wooly-haired, illiterate . . . and phenomenally forbearing." George, Eliza, and their son, Harry, represent another stereotype. Unlike the field hands, who are apparently beyond social redemption or acceptability, George and Eliza suggest the possibility that the only slaves who can effectively undergo a transition from barbarism to civilization are those who are figuratively and literally "unnegroid":

Eliza is a beautiful, pious, hybrid, light enough to pass . . . differing from the genteel mistress who has overseered her education only in the respect that she is a servant. George is darker, but makes up for it by being a mechanical genius, and is, moreover, sufficiently unnegroid to pass through town, a fugitive from his master, disguised as a Spanish gentleman, attracting no attention whatever beyond admiration.

("Everybody's Protest Novel," pp. 16–17)

Stowe's relentless insistence upon categorization leads to, as Baldwin puts it, her "overlooking, denying, evading" the "complexity" of black humanity. She sees her black characters categorically as a problem to be solved. Baldwin attempts to explain why, in fiction as well as in fact, what was once called "the Negro problem" is so uneasily and so inadequately negotiated. He suggests that Americans tend to evade reality, like Stowe seeing only the categorical personifications they wish to see. He considers it a potentially destructive vision based on the fallacious assumption that America is a white country. Baldwin concludes that the spirit of Stowe's faulty vision still holds sway:

... the spirit that breathes in this book, hot, self-righteous, fearful ... is not different from that terror which activates a lynch mob. One need not, indeed, search for examples so historic or so gaudy; this is a warfare waged daily in the heart, a warfare so vast, so relentless and so powerful that the interracial handshake or the interracial marriage can be as crucifying as the public hanging or the secret rape. This panic motivates our cruelty.

("Everybody's Protest Novel," p. 18)

As this passage indicates and as our discussion so far has attempted to demonstrate, Baldwin views the protest novel, the climate out of which it arises, and the assumptions upon which it is based as interrelated phenomena. And in this complex light, he does not feel that good intentions, sincerity, or justifiable moral causes should force us to suspend willingly artistic judgment, especially in the face of "whatever violence they [protest novels] do to language, whatever excessive demands they make of credibility." He realizes that his assessment of the protest novel will be strenuously opposed: "One is told to put first things first, the good of society coming before niceties of style or characterization. Even if this were incontestable—for what exactly is the 'good' of society?—it argues an insuperable confusion, since literature and sociology are not one and the same."

Baldwin's criticism of *Uncle Tom's Cabin* displays his repudiation of everything for which it stands. But, even within the context of this early essay, let alone in later works like *The Fire Next Time*, Baldwin portrays a profound ambivalence toward Stowe and the tradition of the protest novel as a whole. Baldwin's blunt criticism of *Uncle Tom's Cabin* ought to be taken seriously. It is instructive to note how recent critics, who consider *Uncle Tom's Cabin* a positive contribution to American literature and life, respond to Baldwin's own earlier scathing attack. In *Sensational Designs: The Cultural Work of American Fiction, 1790–1860* (1985), Jane Tompkins provides one of the more notable recent critical discussions of *Uncle Tom's Cabin*.[4] Her chapter devoted to the novel, "Sentimental Power: *Uncle Tom's Cabin* and the Politics of Literary History," claims that it "is probably the most influential book ever written by an American."[5] She takes to task Perry Miller, F. O. Matthiessen, Harry Levin, Richard Chase, R. W. B. Lewis, Yvor Winters, and Henry Nash Smith, those patriarchal custodians of the American literary canon, who, she believes, fail to understand the singular significance of Stowe's novel.[6] But Tompkins ignores Baldwin's comments on Stowe in "Everybody's Protest Novel." Yet Baldwin's criticism is more challenging, more polemical, than the relatively genteel critics she cites. The reason why his criticism is not considered lies in a striking parallel between Baldwin's objections to *Uncle Tom's Cabin* itself and a crucial limitation of Tompkins's brand of criticism.

Apart from the difficult and perhaps unanswerable question she raises about the most influential book ever written by an American, she commits, with remarkable extravagance, a critical error analogous to the creative fault that Baldwin discovers at the heart of *Uncle Tom's Cabin*. Baldwin maintains that *Uncle Tom's Cabin* "was not intended to do anything more than prove that slavery was wrong." Tompkins's argument apparently intends to prove that established white male critics have all been wrong about *Uncle Tom's Cabin*. Tompkins attempts to bring an end to the damnation and neglect of women writers. The urgency and the morally justifiable nature of their causes blind both Stowe and Tompkins to crucial aspects of their subjects. In her zeal to prove that slavery was wrong, Stowe fails to present the complex nature of slave humanity. Similarly, Tompkins's own noteworthy cause impels her to overlook or deny the complicated and contradictory nature of

Uncle Tom's Cabin's great popularity and artistic limitation. This does not mean that *Uncle Tom's Cabin* must necessarily be judged in the same critical terms as, say, Herman Melville's *Benito Cereno* or Mark Twain's *The Adventures of Huckleberry Finn*. But how each work succeeds and fails in its own specific depiction of slavery and its consequences is an important question.

Tompkins maintains that a critical comparison of the sort is essentially useless because *Uncle Tom's Cabin* generically distinguishes itself as a "typological narrative." She states, "Therefore, what seem from a modernist point of view to be gross stereotypes in characterization and a needless proliferation of incident, are essential properties of a narrative aimed at demonstrating that human history is a continual reenactment of the sacred drama of redemption."[7] She concludes that Stowe's characters "are not defined primarily by their mental and emotional characteristics—that is to say, psychologically—but soteriologically, according to whether they are saved or damned."[8]

Should "stereotypes" in characterization and "needless proliferation of incident" necessarily be ignored because a writer attempts to portray human history as "a continual reenactment of the sacred drama of redemption"? Tompkins's sense of ideological and canonical urgency leads her to her conclusion. She argues further that *Uncle Tom's Cabin* does not concern slavery as much as it does motherhood. And in this novel light, Stowe becomes something other than the abolitionist whose book was initially written for and serialized in the abolitionist journal *The National Era*; she becomes instead the most celebrated champion of "the new matriarchy."

The novel's deepest political aspirations are expressed only secondarily in its devastating attack on the slave system; the true goal of Stowe's rhetorical undertaking is nothing less than the institution of the kingdom of heaven on earth. . . . In this vision, described in the chapter entitled "The Quaker Settlement," Christian love fulfills itself not in war, but in daily living, and the principle of sacrifice is revealed not in crucifixion, but in motherhood. . . . The home is the center of all meaningful activity; women perform the most important tasks; work is carried on in a spirit of mutual cooperation; and the whole is guided by a Christian woman who, through the influence of her "loving words," "gentle moralities," and "motherly loving kindness," rules the world from her rocking chair.[9]

To be sure, motherhood and the home are central themes in Stowe's attack on slavery. Nevertheless, the dream Stowe presents in "The Quaker Settlement" appears "utopian and arcadian"[10] primarily in the sense that it represents a Christian and antebellum version of the fulfillment of American democratic promise. Thus, Eliza's escape from slavery to freedom becomes as significant as the nature and dynamics of Rachel Halliday's home. Tompkins does not fully address the significance of Stowe's negative portrayal of some of her mothers, especially Marie St. Claire. Even Tompkins's fine reading of the dynamics of sentimentalism in Little Eva's death scene privileges her death in what seems an inappropriate way. Little Eva, after all, is robbed of moral choice. She does not choose to die; she dies of disease. Stowe entitled her novel *Uncle Tom's Cabin* rather than *Little Eva's Heaven* for good reason. But an extended discussion of Uncle Tom's death scene, on the other hand, would lead Tompkins to the heart of the novel, the monstrous evil of slavery, the fact that some white men and women bought and sold black men, women, and children. In "Everybody's Protest Novel," Baldwin realizes that Stowe's treatment of slavery gives the novel an extraordinary power even as he attempts to clarify what he sees as the novel's overwhelming limitation.

Tompkins's interpretation provides a contemporary example of how good intentions and justifiable causes sometimes lead to questionable literary and critical results. In her enthusiasm to correct the critical wrongs committed by established male

critics against women writers, Tompkins commits her own
critical sins of omission and neglect. Her negligence of Baldwin's sharp comments symbolizes her ideological and literary
readiness to exclude and neglect blacks while simultaneously
supporting women and women's rights. Tompkins's omission
is particularly glaring in light of her expressed purpose to study
novels and stories because "they offer powerful examples of a
way a culture thinks about itself, articulating and proposing
solutions for problems that shape a particular historical moment."[11]

This assessment of Tompkins's interpretation does not in-
volve a charge of racism. It concerns rather the very issue she
so eloquently articulates when she castigates white male critics.
Specifically, in matters pertaining to race, just as in consideration of gender, blindness often emerges as the Siamese twin
of extraordinary insight. Consequently, in her reappropriation
and reimagining of the place and meaning of Stowe's novel in
American culture, the lives of the enslaved blacks within the
novel, and by extension all slaves who lived and died, come
across as less important than the careers of those nineteenth-
century white women writers who have been excluded from
serious consideration by the prejudices of white male critics.
Moreover, whatever the function of Stowe's stereotypical de-
pictions in the novel, Tompkins ignores the fact that they have
social as well as literary consequences. In the collective black
mind, "Uncle Tom" now stands as the shuffling personification of obsequiousness and self-hatred, the embodiment of
slavery and the legacy of white supremacy.

Leslie Fiedler's "new" ideas about *Uncle Tom's Cabin* are also
highly problematic.[12] He also argues, though not with Tompkins's polemical zeal, that *Uncle Tom's Cabin* celebrates the
redeeming virtues of motherhood. But Fiedler distinguishes
himself on at least two significant counts. First, he maintains
that works like Stowe's *Uncle Tom's Cabin*; Thomas Dixon, Jr.'s

The Leopard Spots and *The Clansman*; the film *The Birth of a Nation* (D. W. Griffith's adaptation of the Dixon novels); Margaret Mitchell's *Gone With the Wind* (both as a novel and movie), and Alex Haley's phenomenal *Roots* (in all of its popular forms) constitute an American "inadvertent epic."[13] Fiedler states, "Rooted in demonic dreams of race, sex and violence, which have long haunted us Americans, they determine our views of the Civil War, Reconstruction, the rise and fall of the Ku Klux Klan, the enslavement and liberation of African blacks, thus constituting a myth of our history unequalled in scope or resonance by any work of High Literature."[14] Fiedler quotes a passage from Baldwin's "Everybody's Protest Novel" on the negative effect of Stowe's sentimentality, but he effectively dismisses Baldwin's objection by pointing out Baldwin's admission elsewhere that he read the novel over and over as a child. Then Fiedler provides his own interpretation of *Uncle Tom's Cabin*'s influence:

. . . it was Mrs. Stowe who invented American Blacks for the imagination of the whole world. Before *Uncle Tom's Cabin,* they existed as historical, demographic, economic facts, their existence acknowledged but not felt with the passion and intensity we accord what moves through our dreams as well as our waking lives. Afterwards, things were different; Tom, Eliza, and Topsy at least were immediately translated from the pages of Mrs. Stowe's book to the deep psyches of us all, Europeans and Americans, whites and Blacks. . . . these three have survived the fiction in which they appear; becoming, for better or worse, models, archetypal grids through which we perceive the Negroes around us, and they perceive themselves.[15]

Perhaps Fiedler overstates his case. Why would real black people, even though enslaved, have to be "invented" for the "imagination of the whole world"? The popularity of *Uncle Tom's Cabin* was necessarily enhanced by actual historical accounts of the horrors of slavery. Europeans and Northerners frequently traveled throughout the slave states recording brief and extended eyewitness accounts of the slaves—their life and work, religion and superstition, manners and morals, crimes and punishment. One notable example, of course, had been de Tocqueville.[16] During the antebellum period, fugitive and manumitted slaves journeyed throughout New England, Canada, and England, speaking before antislavery societies and telling the story of their bondage and their inspired escapes to freedom; as recent historians have clearly established, slaves themselves were hardly a docile and silent minority. Although forbidden to learn how to read and write, many slaves defiantly refused to remain illiterate. So close, in fact, and so inextricably bound are the quests for freedom and literacy in Afro-American culture, particularly during the antebellum period, that Robert Stepto argues that the dual quest is the quintessential pregeneric myth that underpins all Afro-American literature.[17] Speeches, letters, interviews, and serialized narratives of ex-slaves were regularly published in abolitionist newspapers. Sixty-eight slave narratives were published before the Civil War, thirty-three of them written by blacks themselves. Sixty-seven narratives of former slaves were written after 1860.[18] Thus Stowe could hardly have "invented American Blacks for the imagination of the whole world." The evidence is pervasive. These slave narratives are considerably more than arid historical accounts of the facts and statistics of slavery. It is a well-known fact that Stowe based her portrayal of Uncle Tom on the life of one of them, Josiah Henson.[19] But what has scarcely been commented upon is the degree to which Stowe exploits, with notable literary success, the lives and narratives of other well-known slaves. George Harris's defiant intellectual nature is reminiscent of Frederick Douglass's narrative of 1845. George and Eliza's story parallels, in crucial details, the escape of William and Ellen Craft, who fled to freedom when fair-skinned Ellen cropped her hair and masqueraded as an ailing planter with her faithful and humble servant, William, at her side. Even Cassy's fascinating story appears derived from the complex romantic life of Harriet Jacobs reported in *Incidents in the Life of a Slave Girl*.[20] Stowe, indeed, is known to have read parts of Jacobs's story in manuscript.

When Fiedler refers to Stowe's creation of "archetypal grids through which we perceive the Negroes around us and they perceive themselves," he inadvertently supports and promotes the appropriation of black humanity in the same breath and essay in which he argues against categorical definitions of women's literary works by men.

In the context of our discussion of Baldwin's complex genesis as a writer, the accuracy of Tompkins's and Fiedler's interpretations of *Uncle Tom's Cabin* pales in significance beside their inadvertent or benign neglect of "Everybody's Protest Novel." Whether we agree or disagree with Baldwin's conclusions or claims, the essay remains singularly engaging among discussions of Stowe's novel in this century. Indeed, part of the power of the essay lies in Baldwin's clairvoyant anticipation of the American critics of his future work. This intuitiveness represents the unconscious subtext of his essay. Thus, we witness glimmers of his own fear of being typecast "as *merely* a Negro; or, even, merely a Negro writer." For, once typecast, he perceives that he will be fatally doomed to be interpreted, neglected, or damned by literary and sociological criteria wholly inappropriate to the particular nature of his talent.

This odd combination of intuition and apprehension charges the essay with its polemical vigor and its rhetorical authority. Arguing against the artless fiction of the protest novel, which he takes *Uncle Tom's Cabin* to represent, we observe young Baldwin here impersonating Henry James with an authoritative difference. He is already warring against the threatening possibility of his own vocational limitation—a limitation imposing itself from without and simultaneously corroborating or inscribing itself from deep within. Thus, he comes across rhetorically as the prince par excellence of the disarming assertion—deriving his rhetorical authority from his frequent absolute claims about the human condition. These claims are strung together by precious aperçus no less authoritative. He devotes himself to the revelation of the truth—something he feels Stowe fails to deliver:

> Let us say, then, that truth, as used here, is meant to imply a devotion to the human being, his freedom and fulfillment; freedom which cannot be legislated, fulfillment which cannot be charted. . . . He is not, after all, merely a member of a Society or a Group or a deplorable conundrum to be explained by Science. He is—and how old-fashioned the words sound!—something more than that, something resolutely indefinable, unpredictable. In overlooking, denying, evading his complexity—which is nothing more than the disquieting complexity of ourselves—we are diminished and we perish; only within this web of ambiguity, paradox, this hunger, danger, darkness, can we find at once ourselves and the power to free us from ourselves. It is this power of revelation which is the business of the novelist, this journey toward a more vast reality which must take precedence over all other claims.
>
> ("Everybody's Protest Novel," p. 15)

Dangling rather precariously in this "web of ambiguity, paradox, . . . hunger, danger, darkness," we witness the "disquieting complexity" of Baldwin, the young and unfulfilled artist. "He is not, after all, merely a member of a Society or Group." He is hardly Stowe's Uncle Tom. Yet he is threatened by Uncle Tom's legacy and the tradition of which he is so grandly representative. Baldwin yearns for the power to "find" his true artistic self, a self he ironically wishes to be "resolutely indefinable, unpredictable," in other words, a highly creative self. Consequently, he ends his definition of the human by discussing "this power of revelation." Revelation "is . . . the business of the novelist, this journey toward a more vast reality which must take precedence over all other claims." True artists then must not allow themselves to be defined by any form of categorization that will corrupt their individual views. The tradition of the protest novel corrupts the artistic view—so much so in Stowe's case that Baldwin maintains that Uncle Tom "has been robbed of his humanity and divested of his sex."

Baldwin's objections to Stowe's dehumanization and emasculation of Uncle Tom highlight a deeper concern. To be sure, he devotes his essay to a serious look at the tradition of the American protest novel, past and present, and considers *Uncle Tom's Cabin* the "cornerstone of American social protest fiction." But on another level, Baldwin objects to Stowe's appropriation or, indeed, exploitation of black humanity because he, fledgling novelist, must rescue the image of black America from those who have so profoundly distorted it. Tompkins's and Fiedler's critical readings and evaluations of the book are motivated by canonical ambition, their desire to translate or promote Stowe's novel out of the minority idiom and status of abolitionism and sentimentality to a singular position of its own. Baldwin's concerns reveal the nature of his own ambition. He takes Stowe to task partly because she dares to bother with "the business of the novelist." Such is, according to Baldwin, "beyond Mrs. Stowe's powers" because "she was not so much a novelist as an impassioned pamphleteer." Yet, despite his derogatory comments, Baldwin's attitude toward Stowe is profoundly ambivalent. And his ambivalence characterizes his anxiety about his own work. He stands at a crucial fork in the road. He yearns to become a novelist, but that wish will remain unfulfilled for several years. He takes what he considers a principled artistic stand; he repudiates the tradition of the protest novel.

The polemical tone and rhetorical intensity of Baldwin's remarks clearly suggest a concern more crucial to his immediate life than "a very bad novel" written over a century earlier. "Everybody's Protest Novel" represents the public beginning of his struggle for clarity as a writer. His theoretical perception in this essay supersedes his critical comments on *Uncle Tom's Cabin*. The essay displays his early perception of what happens to the black American when his humanity gets trapped in the web of good ideological intentions, moral self-righteousness, sentimental rhetoric, and misguided thinking—coming from those who are staunch supporters of the principles and promises of democratic life. He prophetically perceives this as his peculiar burden and fate as an American writer, and, therefore, he lashes out at Stowe.

However, even as Baldwin rejects the tradition of protest of which Stowe's *Uncle Tom's Cabin* is so singularly representative, he unconsciously reflects, in his essay, both in tone and in substance, the exhortative rhetoric and aggressive morality of an "impassioned pamphleteer." And despite his apparent indifference to the so-called social "Responsibility" of the novelist, he unconsciously accepts Stowe's own legacy and assumes the responsibility of speaking on behalf of the oppressed.

It is the peculiar triumph of society—and its loss—that it is able to convince those people to whom it has given inferior status of the reality of this decree; it has the force and the weapons to translate its dictum into fact, so that the allegedly inferior are actually made so, insofar as the societal realities are concerned. This is a more hidden phenomenon now than it was in the days of serfdom, but it is no less implacable. Now, as then, we find ourselves bound, first without, then within, by the nature of our categorization. And escape is not effected through a bitter railing against this trap: it is as though this very striving were the only motion needed to spring the trap upon us.

("Everybody's Protest Novel," p. 20)

Baldwin's concern here clearly goes beyond the mere literary. By pointing out the implacable, though superficially various, phenomenon of societal control of those it considers inferior, he speaks as a representative of the oppressed black masses. But as quickly as he moves unconsciously in the direction of Stowe, even alluding to the plight of blacks during slavery, he consciously and polemically veers away. He objects to "categorization" and sees societal definition as a "trap." The tradition of protest fiction, what he calls "a bitter railing against," hardly affords escape. "A bitter railing against" the trap provides the "only motion needed to spring the trap upon us."

The force of Baldwin's attack on Stowe was in part, I believe, an unconscious acknowledgment of the temptations and the impact of her work on his own. *Uncle Tom's Cabin* was, in effect, the hidden mother text conspiring to work itself out in his life and in what would be Baldwin's most widely read and, arguably, his most influential book, *The Fire Next Time*.

There are several significant biographical parallels between Baldwin and Stowe that affected the work of both. Stowe's father, Lyman Beecher, like Baldwin's, was a preacher. And so were six of her brothers.[21] She, of course, was excluded by gender from the ministry, and Baldwin gave up his own child evangelism. But both had grown up in a household where Christianity and a belief in moral righteousness were their daily bread. A century and a decade after the publication of *Uncle Tom's Cabin* in an abolitionist journal, Baldwin published *The Fire Next Time* in two parts, "My Dungeon Shook: Letter to My Nephew on the One-Hundredth Anniversary of the Emancipation" and "Down at the Cross: Letter from a Region in My Mind," the first in *The Progressive* (December 1962) and the second in *The New Yorker* (November 17, 1962). Baldwin, like Stowe in *Uncle Tom's Cabin*, was speaking to the converted. For, if right-minded citizens could see their complex personal connection to the national sin of slavery and racial injustice, perhaps Americans could, in Baldwin's words, "end the racial nightmare, and achieve our country, and change the history of the world."[22]

However, a crucial difference to bear in mind is the tenor of the period during which each writer wrote. The sixties were characterized by democratic and idealistic fervor with a few momentary stays against moral confusion. Its currency of verbal exchange was blunt, direct, exhortative. In poetry, fiction, and certainly in autobiography, the collective temporal urge was to "tell it like it is" and "to let it all hang out." Thus, the excessive sentimentality of Stowe's era, which afforded her readers certain tender mercies of incident, phrasing, and scene, are nonexistent in Baldwin. This difference, however, pales in significance to the similar manner in which they engage their readers. In the end, both Stowe and Baldwin want their readers to *feel right*. After the fashion of preachers, both lecture and exhort their readers on the wages of sins, those sins directly committed and those that are the indirect result of cowardice and moral negligence. The writers connect their literary texts to events of their own era, becoming voices of public conscience—Stowe appealing to the abolitionists and Christians in her audience, Baldwin to liberals and intellectuals, Christians or not.

Stowe and Baldwin employ similar strategies condemning the evils of society, and even the innate depravity of humankind, yet both somehow, rhetorically, excuse the shortcomings of their potential readers even as they abstractly condemn them. In her preface to *Uncle Tom's Cabin,* Stowe writes that the goal of "the artist," is to use "the allurements of fiction" to "breathe a humanizing and subduing influence, favorable to the development of the great principles of Christian brotherhood."[23] "In doing this," Stowe believes, "the author can sincerely disclaim any invidious feeling towards those individuals who, often without any fault of their own, are involved in the trials and embarrassments of the legal relations of slavery. Experience has shown her that some of the noblest of minds and hearts are often thus involved; and no one knows better than they do, that what may be gathered of the evils of slavery from sketches like these is not the half that could be told, of the unspeakable whole" (*Uncle Tom's Cabin,* pp. v–vi). So Baldwin, in what is, in effect, his preface to *The Fire Next Time,* "My Dungeon Shook: Letter to My Nephew on the One Hundredth Anniversary of the Emancipation," also points to the responsibility of whites for cruelty to blacks, but finds them "innocent and well-meaning":

Now, my dear namesake, these innocent and well-meaning people, your countrymen, have caused you to be born under conditions not very far removed from those described for us by Charles Dickens in London of more than a hundred years ago. (I hear the chorus of the innocents screaming, "No! This is not true! How *bitter* you are!")

You were born where you were born and faced the future that you faced because you were black and *for no other reason.* . . . You were not expected to aspire to excellence: You were expected to make peace with mediocrity. Wherever you have turned, James, in your short time on this earth, you have been told where you could go and what you could do . . . and where you could live and whom you could marry.

(*The Fire Next Time,* pp. 20–21)

The writers employ similar rhetorical strategies to persuade their readers. They vividly depict the overwhelming facts of racial injustice. Just as Stowe presents a virtual catalogue of the evils of slavery, Baldwin's *The Fire Next Time* records a twentieth-century urban slavery. He describes what he witnessed during the summer of his fourteenth year in Harlem:

For the wages of sin were visible everywhere, in every wine-stained and urine-splashed hallway, in every clanging ambulance bell, in every scar on the faces of the pimps and their whores, in every helpless, newborn baby being brought into this danger, in every knife and pistol fight on the avenue, and in every disastrous bulletin: a cousin, mother of six, suddenly gone mad, the children parcelled out here and there; an indestructible aunt rewarded for years of hard labor by a slow, agonizing death in a terrible small room; someone's bright son blown into eternity by his own hand; another turned robber and carried off to jail.

(The Fire Next Time, p. 34)

In "Everybody's Protest Novel," Baldwin refers critically to Stowe's "catalogue of violence," which he sees as designed to inspire abolitionism; her book "was not intended to do anything more than prove that slavery was wrong." But Baldwin provides his own colorful and violent collage—the "ambulance bell," the "knife," the "pistol," incarceration, madness, suicide, "children parcelled out here and there." He clearly wishes to prove that the black American dream of freedom has been perpetually deferred. As he says in a new introduction to *Notes of a Native Son:* "There have been superficial changes, with results at best ambiguous and, at worst, disastrous. Morally, there has been no change at all and a moral change is the only real one. '*Plus ça change,* . . . *plus c'est la même chose*'" (*Notes of a Native Son,* p. xiii).

Stowe and Baldwin raise the fundamental issue of the black American's and white American's relationship to God. They warn their readers that the cruel and racist nature of American society mocks God and Christ. Both question why blacks, so horribly victimized, should believe in God at all. When, in *Uncle Tom's Cabin,* George Harris, the escaped slave, is urged by a sympathetic white, to "trust in the Lord," George asks bitterly, "'Is there a God to trust in? . . . Oh, I've seen things all my life that have made me feel that there can't be a God. You Christians don't know how these things look to us. There's a God for you, but is there any for us?'" (*Uncle Tom's Cabin,* p. 130). And Baldwin, relating his personal experience of religious conversion in the summer of his fourteenth year, writes that:

All I really remember is the pain, the unspeakable pain; it was as though I were yelling up to Heaven and Heaven would not hear me.

And if Heaven would not hear me, if love could not descend from Heaven—to wash me, to make me clean—then utter disaster was my portion. . . . And if one despairs—as who has not?—of human love, God's love alone is left. But God—and I felt this even then, so long ago, on that tremendous floor, unwillingly—is white. And if His love was so great, and if He loved all His children, why were we, the blacks, cast down so far? Why?

(*The Fire Next Time*, p. 18)

Stowe uses Augustine St. Claire, the son of a New England "aristocrat" who inherits his slaves, to dramatize most effectively her more sophisticated arguments against slavery. St. Claire is an intelligent and relatively compassionate gentleman trapped in a web of familial and historical circumstances. He is deeply skeptical, even cynical, in his condemnation of the horrors of slavery and of the negligence of well-meaning Christians. St. Claire gives Stowe the opportunity to push her novel beyond the boundary lines imposed by sheer sentimentality and the melodramatic deus ex machina she employs. It is St. Claire, after all, who keeps the self-righteous Christians and "patronizing northerners" honest. His cousin, Miss Ophelia, is the most obvious representative of the type. When he speaks, he addresses, in effect, the reservations and questions about the dilemma of slavery Stowe's readers may have had. His remarks force readers to examine morally where they stand. His method of pedagogy is characterized in turn and sometimes in combination by Socratic doubt and devil's advocacy. Using St. Claire, Stowe makes accessible a series of abstract arguments while simultaneously creating the illusion that such utterances were essentially in accordance with St. Claire's forthright nature.

Marie St. Claire, St. Claire's wife, who is pro-slavery, recounts the wonders of a Sunday sermon in which the text was "He hath made everything beautiful in its season":

"He showed how all the orders and distinctions in society came from God; and that it was so appropriate . . . and beautiful, that some

should be high and some low, and that some were born to rule and
some to serve . . . and he applied it so well to all this ridiculous fuss
that is made about slavery, and he proved distinctly that the Bible
was on our side."

(*Uncle Tom's Cabin*, p. 200)

St. Claire reminds his wife that the religious arguments in
favor of slavery were but sound and fury:

"Religion! Is what you hear at church religion? Is that which can
bend and turn, and descend and ascend, to fit every crooked phase
of selfish, worldly society, religion? Is that religion which is less
scrupulous, less generous, less just, less considerate for man, than
even my own ungodly, worldly, blinded nature? No! When I look
for a religion, I must look for something above me and not something beneath."

(*Uncle Tom's Cabin*, p. 201)

Turning the rhetorical screw even more deeply into her reader's conscience, Stowe continues the debate, this time between
St. Claire and Miss Ophelia. After St. Claire's daughter, little
Eva, dies, he questions his own irresponsibility: " 'What shall
be said of one whose own heart, whose education, and the
wants of society have called in vain to some noble purpose;
who has floated on, a dreamy, mental spectator of the struggles, agonies, and wrongs of man, when he should have been
a worker?' " (*Uncle Tom's Cabin*, p. 336). After Miss Ophelia
replies by urging him to "repent and begin now," he argues:
" 'My view of Christianity is such . . . that I think no man can
consistently profess it without throwing the whole weight of
his being against this monstrous system of injustice that lies
at the foundation of all our society, and if need be sacrificing
himself in the battle.' "

St. Claire is, in a sense, Stowe's eloquent agent of right-
minded rhetoric, since he has never acted according to his
avowed sense of Christian responsibility in a nation where
slavery is legalized. When Miss Ophelia asks St. Claire, "Do
you suppose it possible that a nation will ever voluntarily

emancipate?", his response clarifies the ironies and contradictions reflected in the lives of both Northern Christians and Southern slaveholders. It also raises crucial questions about the future well-being, the fate, of the newly freed slaves:

"But, suppose we should rise up tomorrow and emancipate, who would educate these millions and teach them how to use their freedom. . . . is there enough Christian philanthropy, among your northern states to bear with the process of their education and elevation? . . . If we emancipate, are you willing to educate? How many families in your town would take in a negro man and woman, teach them, bear with them, and seek to make them Christians?"

(*Uncle Tom's Cabin*, p. 338)

Writing one hundred years after Emancipation, Baldwin found himself addressing similar issues in similar terms. *The Fire Next Time*, which includes an extended discussion of the Black Muslim movement, was, in effect, criticism of the failure of Christianity. The aim of Black Muslims, he wrote, was to free themselves from the political tyranny and the religious hypocrisy of white American Christians. The Nation of Islam's basic philosophy was characterized by a passionate belief in separation of the races in the United States. Baldwin described his visit to the Chicago mansion of the Honorable Elijah Muhammad, leader of the Black Muslim sect. In Baldwin's account of how he responded to Elijah Muhammad, he presents himself as a dispassionate and objective observer, weighing the pros and cons of Black Muslim mythology:

For the horrors of the American Negro's life there has been almost no language. . . . And, in fact, the truth about the black man, as a historical entity and as a human being, *has* been hidden from him deliberately and cruelly; . . . Why, then, is it not possible that all things began with the black man and that he was perfect—especially since this is precisely the claim white people have put forward for themselves all these years? Furthermore, it is now absolutely clear that white people are a minority in the world—so severe a minority that they now look rather more like an invention—and they cannot possibly hope to rule it any longer. If this is so, why is it not also possible that they achieved their original dominance through stealth and cunning and bloodshed and in opposition to the will of Heaven, and not, as they claim, by Heaven's will? And if *this* is so, then the sword they have used so long against others can now, without mercy, be used against them.

(The Fire Next Time, pp. 83–84)

By taking the reader through the logic of the Black Muslim theology, by explaining its mythology and then rejecting it with cogent arguments of his own, Baldwin sets the stage for his exhortative closing.

If Uncle Tom symbolizes the monumental dignity and incandescent integrity of a Christian life, so the symbolic Negro is Baldwin's "martyr" in *The Fire Next Time*. The intensity, tone, and indeed the substance of his rhetoric at the essay's end are reminiscent of Stowe's own. It is as though, one hundred years after Emancipation, Stowe returns through Baldwin from her grave to appropriate with extraordinary eloquence the idiom of contemporary America when Baldwin writes:

This past, the Negro's past, of rope, fire, torture, castration, infanticide, rape; death and humiliation; fear by day and night, fear as deep as the marrow of the bone; doubt that he was worthy of life, since everyone around him denied it; sorrow for his women, for his kinfolk, for his children, who needed his protection, and whom he could not protect; rage, hatred, and murder, hatred for white men so deep that it often turned against him and his own, and made all love, all trust, all joy impossible—this past, this endless struggle to achieve and reveal and confirm a human identity, human authority, yet contains for all its horror, something very beautiful. . . .

That man who is forced each day to snatch his manhood, his identity out of the fire of human cruelty that rages to destroy it knows, if he survives his effort, and even if he does not survive it, something about himself and human life that no school on earth—and no church—can teach. He achieves his own authority, and that is unshakable.

(The Fire Next Time, pp. 112–13)

Baldwin concludes his essay with this passionate prophecy:

If we—and now I mean the relatively conscious whites and the relatively conscious blacks, who must, like lovers, insist on, or create,
the consciousness of the others—do not falter in our duty now, we
may be able, handful that we are, to end the racial nightmare, and
achieve our country and change the history of the world. If we do
not now dare everything, the fulfillment of that prophecy, recreated
from the Bible in a song by a slave, is upon us: God gave Noah the
rainbow sign, no more water, the fire next time.

(*The Fire Next Time*, pp. 119–20)

This passage seems to me to reveal the hidden mother text. It
is more than a matter of Baldwin's explicit references to
"prophecy," "a slave," to God and the Bible. It is his direct
appeal to conscience. Here are the final sentences of *Uncle
Tom's Cabin*, the hidden mother text:

A day of grace is yet held out to us. Both North and South have
been guilty before God; and the *Christian Church* has a heavy account to answer. Not by combining together, to protect injustice
and cruelty and making a common capital of sin, is this union to be
saved,—but by repentance, justice and mercy; for, not surer is the
eternal law by which the millstone sinks in the ocean, than that
stronger law by which injustice and cruelty shall bring on nations
the wrath of Almighty God!

(*Uncle Tom's Cabin*, pp. 476–77)

The tone and substance of Stowe's remarks are strikingly similar to Baldwin's. Baldwin predicts that "historical vengeance,
cosmic vengeance" will be inevitable if no change occurs in
America's mind and heart. He warns of "the fire next time."
Stowe warns of "the wrath of Almighty God." Both works are
exhortative pleas for the fulfillment of the extraordinary promises of democracy. Each writer views the black American as
the test of America's achievement of its democratic dream.

In "Everybody's Protest Novel" Baldwin foresees his own
ambivalent position as a polemicist and as a serious novelist.
His early essays bear witness to those paradoxical revelations.

Thus, in his ambitious effort to identify the aesthetic limitations of *Uncle Tom's Cabin*, he brings up Wright's *Native Son*:

Below the surface of this novel there lies, as it seems to me, a continuation, a complement of that monstrous legend it was written to destroy. Bigger is Uncle Tom's descendant, flesh of his flesh, so exactly opposite a portrait that, when the books are placed together, it seems that the contemporary Negro novelist and the dead New England woman are locked together in a deadly, timeless battle; the one uttering merciless exhortations, the other shouting curses. And, indeed, within this web of lust and fury, black and white can only thrust and counter-thrust, long for each other's slow exquisite death.

("Everybody's Protest Novel," p. 22)

It is often stressed that these comments led to Wright's and Baldwin's famous quarrel. This may be partly true. Their personal relationship is somewhat beside the point in the present critical context. Here we look at literary connections. Baldwin views *Native Son* as counterproductive and limited because it is a novel of social protest. Wright, by presenting Bigger Thomas as a symbolic or representative black American, so Baldwin complained, fuels the sentimental love and subconscious hatred of those who viewed blacks as either objects of pity and sympathy or of contempt and scorn. The novel, Baldwin writes, is "a complement of that monstrous legend it was written to destroy." That sort of assessment may seem extreme to readers now, but *Native Son* was published fourteen years before *Brown v. Board of Education of Topeka, Kansas*. There is abundant evidence that the black image in the collective white liberal mind then was reminiscent of the romantic racialism of Stowe's era. The manner in which Baldwin's essay connects Stowe and Wright is striking. In a resonant congruity of metaphorical rhetoric and aesthetic critique, Baldwin discusses the Stowe-Wright connection in terms of interracial intercourse or miscegenation, describing Wright and Stowe as "locked together" in "a web of lust and fury." "Black and white can only thrust and counter-thrust." Stowe, he says, is "uttering merciless exhortations"; Wright is "shouting curses." Bigger, then, is conceived in a century-old totemic bed of misguided racial assumptions and taboos. He is "Uncle Tom's descendant, flesh of his flesh." His fate is prenatally sealed. He will necessarily be a hybrid creature of mixed asethetic blood and uncertain social direction. He will, having been brought so traumatically and stereotypically to life, necessarily hate and murder in his protest against the artistic circumstances of his novelistic debut and also against his dim perception of his own life and death.

It is perhaps an instance of unconscious intent that Baldwin would, in his first published statement on Stowe and Wright, employ a metaphor of miscegenation. Stowe, with her religion of judgment and salvation, is, in a crucial literary sense, Baldwin's dead, white, nineteenth-century mother, and Wright, with his spirit of existential and violent defiance, is Baldwin's contemporary father. Their visions compete to meet "the Negro problem" or "the American dilemma." They leave Baldwin their complex and troubling double legacy.

III "MY ALLY, MY WITNESS, AND ALAS! MY FATHER"

James Baldwin's Response to Richard Wright

When we met, I was twenty, a carnivorous age; he was then as old as I am now, thirty-six; he had been my idol since high school, and I, as fledgling Negro writer, was very shortly in the position of his protégé. This position was not really fair to either of us. As writers we were about as unlike as any two writers could be. But no one could read the future, and neither of us knew this then.

—James Baldwin, "Alas, Poor Richard"

I wanted Richard to see me, not as the youth I had been when he met me, but as a man. I wanted to feel that he had accepted me, had accepted my right to my own vision, my right, as his equal, to disagree with him. . . . And then, so ran the dream, a great and invaluable dialogue would have begun. And the great value of this dialogue would have been not only in its power to instruct all of you, and the ages. Its great value would have been in its power to instruct me, its power to instruct Richard: for it would have been nothing less than that so universally desired, so rarely achieved reconciliation between spiritual father and spiritual son.

—"Alas, Poor Richard"

In *Blues, Ideology, and Afro-American Literature: A Vernacular Theory,* Houston Baker provides a notable assessment of what is often considered Baldwin's ruthless attack on Wright.[1] Focusing on Baldwin's essay "Alas, Poor Richard," published in 1961 shortly after Wright's death, as well as on "Everybody's Protest Novel," published more than a decade earlier, Baker discusses the relation between Wright and Baldwin in the context of his trope of Wright as the black (W)hole.[2]

Baker takes Baldwin, and to a lesser degree Ralph Ellison, to task for their negative evaluations of Wright. From Baker's viewpoint, they invoke the wrong criteria for judgment. He essentially considers their comments as critical instances of "bourgeois" presumption, occasioned by their respective refusal, if not inability, to view and evaluate Wright in terms other than received and clichéd ideas about the nature, quality, and art of fiction. Baker, in effect, attempts to squeeze the complexity of Baldwin's response to Wright into a black (W)hole by characterizing Baldwin's criticism of Wright as "traditional" and, worse, as "malevolent":

In such classic instances of traditional evaluation as James Baldwin's controversial essays and Ralph Ellison's engaging "The World and the Jug," the author of *Native Son* is adjudged a rebellious Southerner psychologically deprived by the Jim Crow ethics of a Mississippi upbringing and intellectually denied by the vagaries of an incomplete formal education. Baldwin insists, for example, in an extraordinarily derogatory postmortem entitled "Alas, Poor Richard" that Wright's "notions of society, politics, and history . . . seemed . . . utterly fanciful." . . . Only at the close of his life, asserts Baldwin, did Wright begin to acquire "a less uncertain esthetic distance, and a new depth." Yet he never achieved, in his successor's venomous accounting, an informed, artistic comprehension of the modern world, remaining through all his days "a Mississippi pickaninny, mischievous, cunning and tough."[3]

Baker's characterization of "Alas, Poor Richard" as "an extraordinarily derogatory postmortem" and "venomous accounting" falls short of his usual critical acumen and magnanimity.[4] His unusually harsh assessment appears less an effort to force Baldwin into his own tropological design than a readiness to focus on the *personal relationship* between Wright and Baldwin as a true reflection of their *literary relationship*. The personal and literary are, needless to say, profoundly and inextricably intertwined. But Baker's stigmatization of Baldwin's evaluation as "malevolent" draws us into the shrouded territory of motivation. It need hardly be said that purity of motive is nonexistent in a writer's life, as it is in the life of a critic or an undertaker. "Alas, Poor Richard," on a closer look, appears to be not "malevolent" at all but a singularly poignant homage.

Baldwin's homage to Wright is that of the black expatriate literary son to his adopted spiritual father. As in his similarly forthright homage to his stepfather in "Notes of a Native Son," so here he seeks to invest a dead man's life "with coherence" and to measure it "with charity." He believes in telling "as much truth as one can bear." Thus, he describes Wright's "lapses, greeds, and errors," like those of his stepfather, with brutal honesty. Take, for example, the "Mississippi pickaninny" passage that moves Baker to his charge of "venomous accounting":

I distrusted his association with the French intellectuals, Sartre, de Beauvoir, and company. I am not being vindictive toward them or condescending toward Richard Wright when I say that it seemed to me that there was very little they could give him which he could use. It has always seemed to me that ideas were somewhat more real to them than people; but, anyway, and this is a statement made with the very greatest love and respect, I always sensed in Richard Wright a Mississippi pickaninny, mischievous, cunning and tough. This always seemed to be at the bottom of everything he said and did, like some fantastic jewel buried in high grass. And it was painful to feel that the people of his adopted country were no more capable of seeing this jewel than were the people of his native land, and were in their own way as intimidated by it.[5]

Is this assessment "extraordinarily derogatory" or "venomous"? On the contrary, Baldwin tells us that he calls Wright "a Mississippi pickaninny" with "the very greatest love and respect." And his admiration shines through when he compares that "Mississippi pickaninny" to "some fantastic jewel buried in high grass" of his Southern nature. Baldwin—given his blackness, his literary ambition, and his relative success— is singularly situated to perceive such things of Wright, of himself. He observes how the French had failed Wright. They fail to see the "fantastic jewel" Baldwin sees. They do not understand or acknowledge the Richard Wright of *Black Boy*. Baldwin is reminded of similar American reactions to Wright. It confirms his own "painful" suspicion that Wright refused to acknowledge a French version of American prejudice.

Baldwin says explicitly throughout "Alas, Poor Richard" that writing about Wright proved to be "a painful and difficult task." It was, to him, in part a duty. Much of the essay reflects Baldwin's homage to Wright, even as he presents his faults and flaws. He focuses on Wright's life in order to clarify aspects of his own life. "Alas, Poor Richard" is Baldwin's public acknowledgment of the significance of Wright to him. He tells us that Wright had been his "idol since high school" and that Wright had strongly recommended him for a Eugene F. Saxton Fellowship. He concedes a crucial difference between Wright's life and his own: "I have not, in my own flesh, traveled, and paid the price of such a journey, from the Deep South to Chicago to New York, to Paris." Furthermore, Baldwin reports that he had made his "pilgrimage" to see Wright because he considered him "the greatest black writer in the world." Wright, then, was living proof that a young black could indeed survive Mississippi and the slums of Chicago and become a writer:

In *Uncle Tom's Children,* in *Native Son,* and, above all, in *Black Boy,* I found expressed, for the first time in my life, the sorrow, the rage, and the murderous bitterness which was eating up my life and the lives of those around me. His work was an immense liberation and revelation for me. He became my ally and my witness, and alas! my father.

("Alas, Poor Richard," p. 153)

Perhaps Baker finds the venom in Baldwin's assessment, later in the essay, as Baldwin begins to view Wright, his former "idol," as an "object lesson." Baldwin reveals that Wright eventually inspires the hatred of most of the black American and African writers who at first admire and emulate him because they believe he despises them. He worries that the same could happen to him one day:

The American Negroes had discovered that Richard did not really know much about the present dimensions and complexity of the Negro problem here, and profoundly, did not want to know. And one of the reasons he did not want to know was that his real impulse toward American Negroes, individually, was to despise them. They, therefore, dismissed his rage and his public pronouncements as an unmanly reflex; as for the Africans, at least the younger ones, they knew he did not know them and did not want to know them, and they despised *him.* It must have been extremely hard to bear, and it was certainly very frightening to watch. I could not help but feeling: *Be careful. Time is passing for you, too, and this may be happening to you one day.*

("Alas, Poor Richard," p. 168)

Baldwin views Wright's present misfortune as a mirror image of his own possible future. And as it turns out, his premonition is well founded. During the late sixties, younger black writers, most notably Eldridge Cleaver, would venomously attack Baldwin himself.[6]

Whatever conclusion we draw about the accuracy or fairness of Baldwin's portrayal, his essay is a valuable literary document. It is a record—deeply subjective and intimate—of one formidable black literary talent observing and reporting on another. When Wright died in 1960, Baldwin had begun to come into his own as a writer. He had published *Go Tell It on the Mountain* in 1953, *Notes of a Native Son* in 1955, and *Giovanni's Room* in 1956.

When Baker turns to Baldwin's specifically literary comments on Wright, he takes the traditional line critics adopt on Baldwin's controversial essays, "Everybody's Protest Novel" and "Many Thousands Gone." But he adds another dimension to the discussion by considering them briefly in the context of Raymond Williams's "bourgeois aesthetic theory":

Baldwin elaborates a contradistinction between *individual* and *society* as though the division possesses the force of natural law, when, in fact, it carries only the reinscribed metaphorical force of an old problematic. The power of the distinction is contingent upon a model of perceiving "reality" that emerges from a peculiar, cultural ordering of existence. And its very delineation, perforce, implies that the person reinscribing its antinomies is superior to all merely *social* determinants. . . .

Bourgeois aesthetics postulates an artistically transcendent realm of experience, production, and value as a "cultural" preserve, a domain where individual creativity ("consciousness") secures itself against corruptions of industrialism ("social being").[7]

This characterization of Baldwin seems appropriate except that in certain crucial ways he errs in his excessive decontextualization of Baldwin's essays and his literary career. To be sure, as Michel Fabre and others have noted, "Everybody's Protest Novel" and "Many Thousands Gone" are marked, at least superficially, by glittering articulateness and apparent disinterested abandonment of the pressing social issues of the day.

Baldwin writes ostensibly about "the business of the novelist" and eschews, even dismisses, a consideration of what is "parroted as his [the writer's] Responsibility" ("Everybody's Protest Novel," pp. 15–16). Furthermore, "Everybody's Protest Novel" was first published in *Partisan Review* (June 1949), at the time America's most cosmopolitan and intellectual journal. The issue in which Baldwin's essay appeared contains articles on Shaw and Pirandello and an exchange on "The Liberal Mind" by Lionel Trilling, Richard Chase, and William Barrett. The editors and writers who were associated with *Partisan Review* viewed themselves as beyond simple categorization. Alfred Kazin describes their milieu:

Kafka, Babel, Joyce, Picasso—not to forget Malraux, Sartre, Italo Svevo, Stravinsky, Schönberg—were the gods of this world to those intellectuals who wanted to be both established and advanced, and soon were. . . .

They saw with the eyes of great twentieth-century masters, Eliot, Yeats, Mann, who were conservative and even artistic. To be a Jew and yet not Jewish; to be of course a liberal, yet to see everything that was wrong with the "imagination of liberalism"; to be Freudian and a master of propriety, academic and yet intellectually avant garde—. . . .[8]

Baldwin's sense of himself certainly echoes something of that set of literary and intellectual assumptions. And it was hardly beneath him to take whatever advantage he could in what he viewed as an enabling context. Nevertheless, Baker's assessment removes Baldwin out of the context of his own hazardous rise from the Harlem ghetto to exceptional literary good fortunes. Baldwin has his own "black blues life"[9]; the bittersweet strains and refrains of it rise up, despite his "bourgeois" declarations and assumptions, between the lines of the essays in which he criticizes Wright. Thus, when Baldwin calls Wright "a Mississippi pickaninny," he indulges his poetic license and provides a moment of black humor. He plays the dozens. Surely he saw a reflection of his own life in Wright's.

And he realized that on some not so inscrutable level he would himself always remain the mischievous and cunning Harlem pickaninny, attempting to display his own precious jewel to a world which insistently and arrogantly intended to categorize him. Referring specifically to this issue, Baldwin informs us in "The Discovery of What It Means to Be an American" that he rediscovered the "pickaninny" in himself while living and writing in Switzerland:

There, in that absolutely alabaster landscape, armed with two Bessie Smith records and a typewriter, I began to try to re-create the life that I had first known as a child and from which I had spent so many years in flight. . . .

Bessie Smith, through her tone and cadence . . . helped me to dig back to the way I myself must have spoken when I was a pickaninny, and to remember the things I had heard and seen and felt. I had buried them very deep.[10]

Baker's discussion does not fully address the complex nature of Baldwin's response to Wright. And it excludes altogether the similarly powerful and enabling force that the life and the writings of Henry James and of Harriet Beecher Stowe contributed to Baldwin, and the similar ambivalence he felt toward them. Consequently, despite its metaphorical beauty and appropriateness, Baker's trope of the black (W)hole seems destined, if Baldwin's relation to Wright sheds any light on the matter, to be compromised by other critical galaxies reflecting individual black artists' individual strengths, weaknesses, and idiosyncrasies. Accordingly, it is to our considerable advantage to examine how Baldwin affirms Wright even as he ostensibly rejects him.

Heretofore, critics, Baker for example, have not thoroughly discussed "Many Thousands Gone."[11] The debate over this essay, as with "Everybody's Protest Novel," has essentially been limited to discussion of its consequence, as a factor leading to the personal falling out between Wright and Baldwin.

Others have agreed or disagreed with Baldwin's critical assessment of the limitations of Wright's *Native Son*.[12] Baldwin never attempts to explain the literary or technical success of *Native Son,* apart from its sensational or representative fleshing out of American racial myths.

Native Son succeeds as a novel because, while Bigger Thomas may only have one controlling or dominant identity, that personality is revealed in a series of well-chosen episodic identities showing hidden aspects of Bigger's self the newspapers would surely miss. *Native Son* is not simply the story, as Baldwin puts it, of an "unremarkable youth" characteristic of "a certain American tradition" ("Many Thousands Gone," p. 31). Nor is Bigger simply a Negro. He is a bullying urban adolescent who accidentally murders, and then becomes a desperate psychopathic murderer again. Once he has been discovered, he becomes a sensational news item and racial scapegoat. But Bigger has his share of quintessential American dreams; he dreams at the novel's beginning of being an aviator and he dreams, near the novel's end, of becoming a great black leader. Baldwin ignores these aspects of Bigger's personality and views him merely as "the incarnation of a myth." Baldwin also fails to acknowledge Wright's masterful use of symbolism, from the novel's opening scene to the closing sound of the door to Bigger's prison cell. And he ignores Wright's symbolic, even prophetic, exploitation of the airplane and news media, those powerful, transforming forces of our time.

Baldwin focuses on the flaws of *Native Son* because he himself refuses to be categorized as "merely a Negro writer." Thus, in "Many Thousands Gone" he uses the persona of an articulate white liberal. We should bear in mind that this is one of Baldwin's earliest essays; for many readers it would be their initial literary encounter with him.[13] Acutely aware of the social climate of the time, he strikes the pose of a thoughtful and knowledgeable white who speaks in a representative tone about the history of race relations in America. This narrative trick is simultaneously a social and literary confidence act. He inspires the confidence of the white reader because he has removed the predictable assumption of black victimization. And because he writes from a perspective outside his own ethnic group, he can presumably see more clearly.

Thus, on a sociocultural level, Baldwin smuggles his ideas across a barrier of prejudicial racial presumptions by conceding to the reader that a white writer is more likely than a black writer to be viewed as an authority figure, even on the matter of race. Baldwin disarms his readers by rhetorically sharing the prejudices of representative white America. Yet he speaks with such perspicacity about the Negro problem because he grew up in the Harlem ghetto. He tells his readers what the inarticulate black ghetto dweller feels and knows white America thinks about the Negro:

One may say that the Negro in America does not really exist except in the darkness of our minds.

This is why his history and his progress, his relationship to all other Americans, has been kept in the social arena. He is a social and not a personal or human problem; to think of him is to think of statistics, slums, rapes, injustices, remote violence; it is to be confronted with an endless cataloguing of losses, gains, skirmishes; it is to feel virtuous, outraged, helpless, as though his continuing status among us were somehow analogous to disease—cancer, perhaps, or tuberculosis—which must be checked, even though it cannot be cured.

("Many Thousands Gone," pp. 24–25)

By referring to the Negro as a sort of walking personification of "slums, rapes, injustices," etc., in the collective white American mind, Baldwin turns another rhetorical screw. He prepares the reader for his extended criticism of Wright's *Native Son,* the primary subject of the essay. By the time Baldwin introduces Wright and *Native Son,* the reader is already privy to a point of view on the Negro question that Baldwin, in the persona of a representative white liberal, considers misguided and dehumanizing.

When Baldwin arrives at that juncture in "Many Thousands Gone," he thinks about his own fate as a black American writer. As he criticizes *Native Son,* his sentences betray a profound ambivalence. Praising Wright as "the most eloquent spokesman" for the "New Negro" who emerged during the twenties and thirties, Baldwin describes *Native Son* as "the most powerful and celebrated statement we have yet had of what it means to be a Negro in America." Nonetheless, Baldwin, who had not yet published his own first novel, considers misguided any novelist who is "committed to the social struggle." Indeed, there are evocations of James and Stowe throughout this section of the essay. Even as he composes a unique and memorable essay, one as valuable for its own social as well as its literary analysis, he embraces a Jamesian notion of the writer, as "artist" (he does not use the word "writer"). And the artist, as Wright he argues does not, must recognize that "the reality of man as a social being is not his only reality."

In "Many Thousands Gone," Baldwin attempts to make a crucial distinction between Wright's point of view as a writer and his own. While writing an essay that focuses on black experience and the problem of recording that experience, Baldwin has set for himself what he apparently considers loftier literary goals. "That artist is strangled," he wrote, "who is forced to deal with human beings solely in social terms; and who has, moreover, as Wright had, the necessity thrust on him of being the representative of some thirteen million people. It is a false responsibility (since writers are not congressmen) and impossible, by its nature, of fulfillment" ("Many Thousands Gone," p. 33). Yet Baldwin faces a dilemma. He speaks as a congressman would when he addresses, in the introductory section of the essay, the historical plight and the mythic image of the black American in the white mind. Even when

he makes points or raises objections that are specifically literary, like the fatal flaw of *Native Son*, he projects a social
message that is closely akin to Wright's. And this narrative
manifestation of conscious repudiation and unconscious affir-
mation gives the essay its striking rhetorical power.

The artistic flaws of *Native Son*, Baldwin thought, center
around Wright's attempt "to redeem a symbolic monster in
social terms." Bigger Thomas, of course, is the "symbolic monster"; he represents "the incarnation of a myth." In a 1984
interview, Baldwin, while confessing that Stowe and *Uncle
Tom's Cabin* were his primary targets, defended what he called
his "technical objection" to "Fate," the final section of *Native
Son*:

I could not accept the performance of the lawyer at the end of the
book. . . . I think it was simply absurd to talk about this monster
created by the American public and then expect the public to save
it! Altogether, I found it too simple-minded. Insofar as the American
public creates a monster, they are not about to recognize it. You
create a monster and you destroy it.[14]

This opinion explains why in "Many Thousands Gone" Baldwin calls the lawyer Max's closing courtroom argument in the
defense of Bigger "one of the most desperate performances in
American fiction." If, according to Baldwin, Bigger had been
more recognizably human—more akin in behavior, thought,
and social adjustment to his friends and members of his
family—social redemption might have made artistic sense. But
Wright refuses to make Bigger human by failing "to convey
any sense of Negro life as a continuing and complex group
reality." The reader knows as little about Bigger at the end of
the novel as he knows at the beginning, Baldwin maintains,
and hence the other black characters—Bigger's friends and
family—"might be considered as far richer and far more subtle
and accurate illustrations of the ways in which Negroes are
controlled in our society and the complex techniques they have

evolved for their survival." Wright's failure to show or highlight this complex intragroup dynamic, "that depth of involvement and unspoken recognition of shared experience," robs
the novel of its potential revelatory force:

> What this means for the novel is that a necessary dimension has been
> cut away. . . . It is this which creates its climate of anarchy and un-
> motivated and unapprehended disaster; and it is this climate, com-
> mon to most Negro protest novels, which has led us all to believe
> that in Negro life there exists no tradition, no field of manners, no
> possibility of ritual or intercourse. . . . But the fact is not that the
> Negro has no tradition but that there has as yet arrived no sensibility
> sufficiently profound and tough to make this tradition articulate.
>
> ("Many Thousands Gone," pp. 35–36")

Baldwin reminded the reader, and the nation, that Afro-
American experience, despite poverty and oppression, is rich
and complex. In that light, his position reminds one of
Wright's. To interpret, promote, and celebrate the tradition of
the Negro is the task of a spokesman, one, to use Baldwin's
description of Wright, "clearly committed to the social struggle." But Baldwin's unconscious identification with Wright,
throughout the essay, underscores his ambivalence. When he,
for example, lists the things—"no tradition, no field of manners, no possibility of ritual or intercourse"—he simultaneously refers to Henry James's itemization of absent things
in American life and Wright's list in *Black Boy* of crucial ab-
sences in black American life.[15] By invoking James in his criticism of Wright, Baldwin strongly suggests that he identifies
with James. But even this conscious association is deeply complicated by his double consciousness, the dual nature of his
experiences as a black American, artist and citizen. Thus, while
Baldwin invokes James, he focuses on the presumed absence
of things in *Afro-American life,* contradicting Wright, who suggests in *Black Boy* that black Americans and black American
culture are shallow and impoverished:

I used to mull over the strange absence of real kindness in Negroes, how unstable our tenderness, how lacking in genuine passion we were, how void of great hope, how timid our joy, how bare our traditions, how hollow our memories, how lacking we were in those intangible sentiments that bind man to man, and how shallow was even our despair. . . . And when I brooded upon the cultural barrenness of black life, I wondered if clean, positive tenderness, love, honor, loyalty, and the capacity to remember were native with man.[16]

Baldwin does not share Wright's bleak estimation of black American culture. He focuses on the failure of its writers to articulate its complex nature and positive attributes: "But the fact is not that the Negro has no tradition but that there has as yet arrived no sensibility sufficiently profound and tough to make that tradition articulate." Wright is Baldwin's immediate target; however, he implicitly insists upon distinguishing himself among all American writers who have written of the Negro. His quest, at this initial and willful moment in his career, is for an original and previously unoccupied literary space. Even if it was true that no single writer had yet existed whose sensibility was "sufficiently profound and tough" to articulate the American Negro experience; even if Douglass, Du Bois, and Hughes had not preceded him, nor Melville, Twain, and Faulkner, Baldwin would be driven to write about blacks in terms of the overwhelming consequences of racial consciousness and prejudice. This fact alone, despite his public outcry against Wright and *Native Son* and despite his quasi-Jamesian aesthetics, brings him closer to Wright than he, at the outset of his career, can consciously acknowledge or accept. His acceptance of Wright's literary legacy would include the recognition that whoever presumes to articulate the black American tradition would necessarily face black America's historical rage as well as its monumental fortitude.

Thus, in the context of this very essay, Baldwin, in effect, becomes a spokesman for the collective rage of black Americans in a way Bigger Thomas cannot. While deploring the

notion of Bigger's murder of Mary Dalton as an "act of creation," Baldwin, ironically given his judgment of Wright,
writes:

And there is, I should think, no Negro living in America who has
not felt, briefly or for long periods, with anguish sharp or dull, in
varying degrees and to varying effect, simple, naked and unanswerable hatred; who has not wanted to smash any white face he may
encounter in a day, to violate, out of motives of the cruelest vengeance, their women, to break the bodies of all white people and
bring them low, as low as that dust into which he himself has been
and is being trampled; no Negro, finally, who has not had to make
his own precarious adjustment to the "nigger" who surrounds him
and to the "nigger" in himself.

(*"Many Thousands Gone,"* p. 38)

Baldwin speaks as Bigger Thomas would if Bigger's hatred for
whites had not been, according to Wright's narrator, "dumb,
cold, and inarticulate."[17]

While Baldwin criticizes Wright harshly for a failure of artistic imagination and debunks his presentation of Bigger as
the "incarnation of a myth" and as the product of an oppres-
sive environment, Baldwin demonstrates that he, like Wright,
is willing to speak eloquently on behalf of the suffering black
masses. However, there is a crucial difference between Wright
and Baldwin and it involves Baldwin's belief in the democratic
necessity and possibility of widespread interracial communication, harmony, and love. When he uses "we" or "our" in
referring to the racial situation in the United States, he suggests the profound and unacknowledged interconnections of
America's interracial past as well as the inexorability of its
complex interracial fate.

When, in "Many Thousands Gone," Baldwin takes a hard
look at the failure of *Native Son,* he focuses on certain technical
matters like Max's long defense of Bigger Thomas at the novel's
end. But his quarrel with Wright really centers on the encom-
passing issue of literary vision. He disagrees with Wright be-

cause he feels that the path Wright has taken (*Native Son* being the overwhelming indication of the choice) will severely limit him. Baldwin believes he will become "merely a Negro writer." "Many Thousands Gone" is designed to show the reader the dead end to which Wright's sense of literary and social vision leads, yet it demonstrates Baldwin's own complicated ambivalence toward the man he describes later as his literary "father." The essay also tangentially shows his attraction to the respective visions of James and Stowe about the American writer's role, with the presence and point of view of each writer in his imagination checking and balancing the other. He refers to the Afro-American's "paradoxical adjustment which is perpetually made." He cannot totally embrace James because the racial issue leads him directly to Wright and *Native Son*. And although he is powerfully attracted to Wright's socioliterary power, the message is one of black rage. And thus, he shifts toward Stowe, albeit not intentionally.

Baldwin's will to power as a writer predisposes him to misread Wright, although his misreading of *Native Son* is extraordinarily perceptive. Yet in the end the essay tells us as much—via its ambivalent rhetorical flourishes, the content of its argument, the unambiguous source of that content—about young Baldwin, the unfulfilled novelist and future spokesman, and thus leader, of black Americans, as it does about Wright and *Native Son*. "Many Thousands Gone" is one of his first imaginative, though expository, attempts to escape or negate the power of *Native Son*. Baldwin sees Wright as the latest literary victim, the most famous and successful example of a Negro writer who has been compromised creatively and professionally by race. He places him in the footsteps of the earlier writers of Negro protest fiction. And the younger writer fears a similar fate. These early essays are the signs of his personal struggle to avoid becoming "*merely* a Negro; or, even, merely a Negro writer."

Throughout Baldwin's career, one can turn from his major essays and find episodic renderings of their central ideas in his works of fiction. It is as though each literary artifact has a life of its own but lives in an enlightening symbiotic relationship with the other genre. Thus, as demonstrated earlier, *Notes of a Native Son* can be read as a theoretical blueprint of Baldwin's literary career. We can, for example, move from Baldwin's critical comments on *Native Son* in "Everybody's Protest Novel" and "Many Thousands Gone" to instances in his fiction where *Native Son* is clearly on his mind. At the beginning of his career, preoccupied with Wright's novel, he expresses a revisionary urge in which he tries, in repeated ingenious turns, to negotiate and thereby mitigate or transform the black rage of *Native Son*.

"Previous Condition" is an example of such early revisionary creativity.[18] Appearing in 1948, a year before "Everybody's Protest Novel" and three years before "Many Thousands Gone," "Previous Condition" is Baldwin's first published short story. It appeared in *Commentary*. On the surface, "Previous Condition" depicts the rage and desperation of Peter, an unemployed black actor. However, in this early attempt at fiction, Baldwin strains to avoid what he considers the imaginative failure of *Native Son,* and thus to move beyond Wright. Yet *Native Son* directly influences aspects of the story's central theme and general tone. "Previous Condition" explores the devastating emotional impact of Peter's questionable financial and professional circumstances and his failure, because of racial discrimination, to find adequate housing. Choosing to live in downtown Manhattan rather than Harlem, Peter is repeatedly rebuffed and rejected by landlords. And after a Jewish friend rents a room for him, the landlord discovers that his real tenant is black and angrily evicts him, instructing him to go back to Harlem.

The opening of the story reminds one of *Native Son*'s beginning. Like Bigger Thomas, Peter awakens in a single room when he hears the ringing of his neighbor's alarm clock. Peter's room, like the one-room southside apartment of the Thomases, is depressing; it is "the kind of room that defeated you." But even as Baldwin recalls the very beginning of *Native Son*, he struggles to write his own unique story. Thus, Peter is unemployed, but he accepts and rejects the roles he will play on the basis of principled professional self-definition. Bigger Thomas's alarm clock awakens him to a segregated black world of poverty and defeat. Peter dares to occupy a space previously untenanted by blacks. He does this at considerable risk. The alarm clocks he hears ringing are those of his white neighbors—symbolically warning him of their proximity and reminding him of his fitful isolation. As Baldwin strives forcefully to give his story a life of its own, he returns compulsively to Wright's themes and characters.

Baldwin quickly introduces characters reminiscent of the principal characters in *Native Son*. Peter, despite the ostensible difference, is Baldwin's Bigger Thomas. He, like Bigger, has no father for guidance. And he is similarly contemptuous of his mother's situation. Before he runs away from home at sixteen, the family lives in New Jersey in "an old shack . . . in the nigger part of town." And Peter confesses, "I hated all the people in my neighborhood. They went to church and they got drunk. They were nice to white people. When the landlord came around, they paid him and took his crap." Bigger Thomas's mother, in exasperation and anger, calls her son "dumb, black, and crazy" (*Native Son,* p. 12). Peter's mother tells him, "'You ain't never gonna be nothing but a bum.'" Jules Weisman, like Jan Erlone and Max in *Native Son,* represents the good-intentioned white. Finally, Ida, Peter's part-time married lover, has the same attitude toward Peter as Mary Dalton toward Bigger.

As Baldwin rehearses Wright's cast of major characters, his

revisionary turns reveal an aggressive struggle to create and maintain his own angle of literary vision. Throughout "Previous Condition," Baldwin dramatizes his primary objection to Wright's portrayal of Bigger Thomas. He attempts, in essence, to make Peter reflect what he calls in "Many Thousands Gone" the black American's "paradoxical adjustment." This peculiar form of social and psychological adjustment involves the black American's necessary acceptance of what Baldwin describes as "his private Bigger Thomas living in the skull." Baldwin concludes in "Many Thousands Gone": "Only this recognition sets him [the Negro] in any wise free and it is this . . . which lends to Negro life its high element of the ironic." Peter, unlike Bigger Thomas, adjusts to his situation with a studied, methodical approach. He repeatedly plays roles in real life that he would flatly refuse as a professional:

In all this running around I'd learned a few things. Like a prizefighter learns to take a blow or a dancer learns to fall, I'd learned how to get by. . . . When I faced a policeman I acted like I didn't know a thing. I let my jaw drop and I let my eyes get big. . . . I took a couple of beatings but I stayed out of prison and I stayed off the chain gang.

("Previous Condition," p. 73)

In "Many Thousands Gone," Baldwin stresses that adjustment must be "perpetually made." In his characterization of Peter in "Previous Condition" he allows Peter to think out loud about how he feels after the eviction. When his Jewish friend, Jules, asks him if he put up a fight, he tells him he wants a place to sleep "without dragging it through the courts," an obvious reference to Max's lengthy defense of Bigger in *Native Son*. Peter's comments might have been uttered by Bigger Thomas if Bigger had been more articulate. He complains resentfully to Jules, " 'I've been fighting so goddamn long I'm not a person anymore. I'm not Booker T. Washington. I've got no vision of emancipating anybody. I want to emancipate myself. If this goes on much longer . . . I'll blow my top, I'll break somebody's head. I'm worried about what's happening to me, *to me* inside!' "

Peter is almost driven insane by his internal rage. And he, like Bigger, may be inclined to "break somebody's head." But instead he, for the most part, maintains a sense of personal dignity and grace under the pressure. Baldwin, here in his professional debut as a creative writer, does not wish to type-cast his characters as mere social creatures whose actions are predetermined by America's legal and customary racial restrictions. Although Peter claims "hatred had corrupted me like cancer in the bone," he tries to overcome his racial "fate" by insisting upon the specific nature of his suffering as an individual. He wants "to emancipate" *himself.* This process of self-definition and self-emancipation involves taking certain principled risks, regardless of the cost, in order to achieve that inviolate sense of personal freedom.

In light of the preceding, Baldwin rolls out his heaviest revisionary artillery. Peter, the unemployed actor, is offered the lead roll in a movie of *Native Son.* He and Ida, his solicitous companion, discuss the matter:

"Metro offered me a fortune to come to the coast and do the lead in *Native Son* but I turned it down. Type casting, you know, it's so difficult to find a decent part."

"Well, if they don't come up with a decent offer soon tell them you'll go back to Selznick. He'll find you a part with guts—the very *idea* of offering you *Native Son!* I wouldn't stand for it."

("Previous Condition," pp. 79–80)

This scene corroborates Baldwin's preoccupation with *Native Son* and its threatening symbolic force. We can see how Peter's rejection of the role allows him the personal freedom to wait for "a decent offer" or "a part with guts." His personal attempt "to emancipate" himself is inextricably linked to his professional ambition to realize the specific nature and promise of his individual talent, not as a mere Negro actor. Baldwin attempts to write his own story here by rejecting the doctrine and limitations of *Native Son*, and, like Peter, by occupying a previously untenanted and preferably a nonracialized space, to choose the books he writes, the characters he creates, on the basis of his own artistic vision rather than America's racial prescriptions. His stance represents a powerful yearning for originality. Wright, returning from Paris, insisted on playing the role of Bigger Thomas when *Native Son* was produced as a movie. Baldwin implicitly suggests or hints at a more pernicious social effect or corrupting influence of the book; the fact that a distinguished writer, and an inexperienced actor, would be allowed to play such a role seems to corroborate Baldwin's claim in "Many Thousands Gone" that Bigger Thomas is essentially "the incarnation of a myth."

Peter remains ironically a victim of the private Bigger Thomas in his skull. As Ida and Peter have a few drinks in a restaurant and continue their polite conversation over dinner, Ida solicitously advises, " 'We're all in this together, the whole world. Don't let it throw you.' " She adds later, " 'In all of Europe there's famine and disease, in France and England they hate the Jews—nothing's going to change.' " This moment is reminiscent of Bigger's initial encounter with Jan Erlone when he and Mary insist upon treating Bigger as though he were not their chauffeur. By allowing Ida to mouth platitudes about universal suffering, Baldwin highlights her failure to see the individual black American across the table from her. Peter resents her patronizing tone and changes the ambience by joking irreverently: " 'I'm gonna go back to my people where I belong and find me a nice, black nigger wench and raise me a flock of babies.' " Ida raises her fork and raps him maternally across his knuckles. Peter's private Bigger Thomas unexpectedly erupts: "I screamed and stood up screaming and knocked the candle over: 'Don't do that, you bitch, don't ever do that!' " Ida grabs the candle, her face "perfectly white," and tells him to sit down. "Everyone was looking at us . . . a black boy and a white woman alone together. I knew it would take nothing to have them at my throat."

The scene reminds one of Bigger Thomas's fear and impulsiveness that fateful night in Mary Dalton's bedroom. Furthermore, as mentioned earlier of "Notes of a Native Son," Baldwin has had his own fit of unexpected rage, hurling a water mug at a white waitress who refuses to serve him in Trenton. He concludes on that occasion that he could have murdered or could have been murdered. This shock of recognition forces Baldwin to reflect on the consequences of violence and bitterness in his life and in his art. But in this first short story Baldwin fails to resolve his creative dilemma. While rejecting *Native Son* as an appropriate model and Bigger Thomas as a quintessential black character, he has trouble creating an original space for himself. Thus, Peter is caught significantly between polarities, between the white world and the black, between the actor's need to define himself through performance and his need to realize himself through appropriately significant roles.

After dinner, Peter returns to Harlem, presumably in search of a sustaining community where he will be neither rejected nor evicted. He returns to his "previous condition," to the symbolic world of his fugitive father and impoverished mother, because he has no other place to go. The climactic end of Baldwin's first effort at fiction suggests that he, like Peter, will have trouble finding a "decent offer," a professional role of unambiguous integrity and a home where his race will be insignificant. It also suggests the themes that will dominate Baldwin's career, eventually determining his personal as well as professional fate: the individual versus the family and community; the romantic and social relationships between blacks and whites; the artist versus the ambivalent self and the conspiring world. Like Peter in "Previous Condition," Baldwin

will be driven to return home to Harlem by vast and impersonal circumstances beyond his control. The story ends when
Peter enters a black bar in Harlem and offers to buy two black
women a drink. The streetwise women are puzzled by the
young man's generosity and motives. The older woman asks
him, "'What's your story?'" Peter's reply is the story's closing
line: "'I got no story, ma.'" Just as Peter refuses to be typecast
and play Bigger Thomas and hence remains unemployed, so,
at the outset of his career, Baldwin struggles to find an appropriate role and space for himself as a writer who just happens to be a Negro.

In "Previous Condition," Baldwin strives to get around *Na-
tive Son* even as he imitates it. "This Morning, This Evening,
So Soon" is a more subtle rendition but nonetheless revealing.
Published twelve years after "Previous Condition" (but not in
a book until collected in *Going to Meet the Man* in 1965), "This
Morning, This Evening, So Soon" is the story of a black American singer/actor who makes it big in Paris. He is especially
noted for his role as Chico in a movie entitled *Les Fauves Nous
Attendent*. Chico, the son of a Martinique woman and a
French *colon* who hates his mother and his father, has fled to
Paris, "carrying his hatred with him." Baldwin writes that Chico's hatred "has now grown, naturally, to include all dark
women and all white men, in a word, everyone. He descends
into the underworld of Paris, where he dies. Les fauves—the
wild beasts—refers to the life he has fled and to the life which
engulfs him." He is an international variation of Bigger
Thomas. He, too, allows hatred to destroy him. Baldwin's
protagonist, who is never named, in stark contrast to Chico is
a successful black actor, happily married to Harriet, a beautiful
Swedish woman. The story begins the day before the actor,
his wife, and their son are to return to America. The opening
line, "'You are full of nightmares,'" as Harriet tells her nos-

talgic but apprehensive husband, underscores the basic sub-
plot of the story. The nightmare is the nameless protagonist's
earlier history, his memory of racial discrimination in the
United States. He is, despite his success and his happy marriage, still, and perhaps forever, trapped in his history because
that history is trapped in him. For his twelve years in Paris,
he has kept the wild beasts of his nightmares at bay. The story
is a revision of *Native Son*, with the interracial hatred and
violence of *Native Son* replaced with a singular example of
enduring interracial and international love. This glimpse of a
life, in a cosmopolitan setting free of the effects of racial prejudice, illuminates the provincial character of race relations in
America. The narrator tells us early on, as he silently caresses
his wife, that he had had to leave home to find happiness:

If I had never left America, I would never have met her and would
never have established a life of my own, would never have entered
my own life. . . . If Harriet had been born in America, it would have
taken her a long time, perhaps forever, to look on me as a man like
other men; if I had met her in America, I would never have been
able to look on her as a woman like all other women. The habits of
public rage and power would also have been our private compul-
sions, and would have blinded our eyes. We would never have been
able to love each other. And Paul would never have been born.

(*Going to Meet the Man*, pp. 127–28)

Baldwin's narrator laments the American form of socializa-
tion and social categorization, the "habits of public rage and
power" that lock the individual within the circumscribed limits
of race: "For, everyone's life begins on a level where races,
armies, and churches stop." The words remind us of Baldwin's
criticism of *Native Son*, in which Bigger is presented not as a
man but rather as a monstrous "incarnation of a myth."

Blindness is a central theme in *Native Son*. Mrs. Dalton is
literally blind. And the name Dalton suggests Daltonism, a
form of color blindness. The Daltons, essentially slum lords,
who make their money by robbing their segregated black ten-

ants blind, are, in turn, blinded by their "public power." They cannot see Bigger Thomas. So, the narrator in Baldwin's story believes that America, in preventing the relationship between him and his wife, Harriet, would have "blinded" their eyes.

After Bigger's existentially redemptive murder of Mary Dalton, Wright wrote:

> The thought of what he had done, the awful horror of it, the daring associated with such actions, formed for him for the first time in his fear ridden life a barrier of protection between him and a world he feared. He had murdered and created a new life for himself. It was something that was all his own, and it was the first time in his life he had had anything that others could not take from him.
>
> (*Native Son*, p. 101)

But Baldwin sees this murder not as a redemption but as a hopeless response. In "This Morning, This Evening, So Soon," Baldwin first removes his couple from a context of public rage and racial fear, protecting them from the socio-sexual myths that surround the relationship in America between black men and white women, and thus between Bigger and Mary. He explores the private consequences of shared moments of tenderness between a black man and a white woman. But even at this revisionary turn, Baldwin displays his ambivalent attraction to Wright. He recalls how Wright's narrator describes Bigger Thomas after his murder of Mary. Thus, even as Baldwin substitutes public fear with the private serenity of individual hearts, as he replaces Wright's gory violence with a passionate scene of emotional consummation, both the rhetoric and the substance of the story reveal that his protagonist, like Bigger, is fated to remain a native son. Baldwin's protagonist and Harriet fall in love in Paris, he for the first time, on the Port Royal Bridge "one tremendous April morning." Unlike the winter scene in Mary Dalton's bedroom where "hazy blue light . . . seeps into the room," it is a fine spring day. "The sun fell over everything, like a blessing . . ."

During all the years of my life, until that moment, I had carried the menacing, the hostile, killing world with me everywhere. No matter what I was doing or saying or feeling, one eye had always been on the world . . . that world on which I knew one could never turn one's back, the white man's world. And for the first time in my life, I was free of it; it had not existed for me; I had been quarreling with my girl. It was our quarrel, it was entirely between us, it had nothing to do with anyone else in the world.

(*Going to Meet the Man*, pp. 135–36)

Baldwin's love scene here, even with its cosmopolitan flourishes, is deeply influenced by *Native Son*. The fear that miraculously disappears is a socially determined fear, a learned American response. Wright focused on that fear by placing Bigger in the unprecedented context of a white woman's bedroom, violating the social taboo. Black American men and white American woman, in slavery and after emancipation, were, by law and custom, forbidden to consort. Baldwin's story offers a cosmopolitan variation on this old American theme.

As spelled out in "Many Thousands Gone," Baldwin believes that Wright made an artistic mistake by portraying Bigger as so out of touch with his own humanity that only murder could suggest the possibility of redemption. In "This Morning, This Evening, So Soon," Baldwin's protagonist will not murder his girl. The two lovers marry and become the proud parents of a son. The protagonist's elation comes not from murder, as it does with Bigger's, but from liberation from racially motivated fear and humiliation:

For the first time in my life I had not been afraid of the patriotism of the mindless, in uniform or out, who would beat me up and treat the woman who was with me as though she were the lowest of untouchables. For the first time in my life I felt that no force jeopardized my right, my power, to possess and to protect a woman; for the first time, the first time, felt that the woman was not, in her own eyes or in the eyes of the world, degraded by my presence.

(*Going to Meet the Man*, p. 136)

And yet the sense of glorious personal freedom represents a beginning rather than an end. His bitter memories of American racial discrimination will reassert themselves at unexpected moments like capricious and ferocious wild beasts. As with Peter in "Previous Condition," so the actor/singer in "This Morning, This Evening, So Soon" bears out Baldwin's extraordinary conclusion in *Notes of a Native Son:* "No American Negro exists who does not have his private Bigger Thomas living in the skull." Vidal, the French director, and his black American star quarrel over the appropriate manner in which Chico should play a scene. It leads to a sharp personal exchange:

"I am a French director who has never seen your country. I have never done you any harm, except, perhaps, historically—I mean, because I am white—but I cannot be blamed for that—"

"But I can be," I said, "and I am! I've never understood why, if I have to pay for the history written in the color of my skin, *you* should get off scot-free!" But I was surprised at my vehemence, I had not known I was going to say these things.

(*Going to Meet the Man,* p. 147)

The scene, referring to the black history "written in the color" of the American actor's skin, places race at the center of the quintessential American notion of identity. Vidal warns the black American actor:

"I beg you not to confuse me with the happy people of your country, who scarcely know that there is such a thing as history and so, naturally, imagine that they can escape, as you put it, scot-free . . . you are not talking to Jean Luc Vidal, but to some other white man.

(*Going to Meet the Man,* pp. 147–48)

Even as Baldwin attempts to revise *Native Son,* as he replaces Bigger Thomas's brutality and violence with his protagonist's color-blind romance, the black American actor is still victimized by unexpected eruptions of racial bitterness. Consequently, Baldwin's idealized interracial relationship, flourishing in another culture and another country, is simultaneously an expression of his yearning for a conciliatory and harmonious integration of the races and an indictment of American racial bigotry. It is a fictionalized version of "Many Thousands Gone." Like it, the story highlights his own ambivalent complexity about himself as a black writer and a man who is not "merely" a Negro. "This Morning, This Evening, So Soon" affirms aspects of Wright's literary vision even as it criticizes them. Baldwin exploits Stowe's idea of fiction as a vehicle of moral suasion even as he demonstrates the crippling limitations of racial categorization. And he shows how Henry James's view of the American as a new man is complicated by the "history written in the color" of one's skin. Whether at home or abroad, the black American remains, implacably or inescapably, in Baldwin's words, "the interloper," "the bastard of the West," "the stranger in the village."

Furthermore, despite Baldwin's Jamesian syntax, the substance and the rhetoric of his prose reflect the merged energy of resentment and conciliation that characterizes the lives of the dispossessed and disesteemed. Like the poignant ring of racial agony and promise one hears in "Notes of a Native Son," Baldwin writes here, and will rewrite in all the rest of his essays and his fiction, the mournful music of loss and invisibility, but also the compelling chords of fortitude.

IV THE "BITTER NOURISHMENT" OF ART

The Three Faces on James Baldwin's Mountain

As the singing filled the air the watching, listening faces underwent a change, the eyes focusing on something within; the music seemed to soothe a poison out of them; and time seemed, nearly, to fall away from the sullen, belligerent, battered faces, as though they were fleeing back to their first condition, while dreaming of their last.

—James Baldwin, "Sonny's Blues"

Harriet Beecher Stowe, Richard Wright, and Henry James converge and assert themselves with hidden force and wonder in Baldwin's first novel, *Go Tell It on the Mountain*. Baldwin tries to deliver the aesthetic promise of "Everybody's Protest Novel" and "Many Thousands Gone." Stowe, Wright, and James dwell, like holy ghosts, in the subterranean interstices of Baldwin's text. While no full accounting can be given here of the three writers' profound presence in the novel, or of the other writers who lie beneath the surface of Baldwin's novel, it is strikingly reminiscent of James Joyce's *A Portrait of the Artist as a Young Man*; John Grimes is like Stephen Daedalus—both are young artists, both troubled by their religious heritage. And it resembles Nathaniel Hawthorne's *The Scarlet Letter*. After all, Elizabeth in *Go Tell It on the Mountain* has an illegitimate son, John, whose father remains (to the novel's other characters) anonymous. Like Hester, Elizabeth maintains her dignity and pride, for like Hester, her illegitimate act had "a consecration of its own." The Reverend Gabriel Grimes, like the Reverend Arthur Dimmesdale, lives guilty with his own secret sin of adultery. And near the end of the novel as John lies "possessed" on "the threshing floor" of the church, he envisions his mother in a grave "dressed in scarlet."

But Wright and James, and to a lesser degree Stowe, are the focal points. I merely hint at the complexity of James's aesthetic vision here since a more thorough analysis is provided in the next chapter. Stowe is the "impassioned pamphleteer," advocating the redemptive power of Christianity; Wright symbolizes the tradition of black protest fiction with black rage and gratuitous violence; and James represents Baldwin's ideal artist. Baldwin tries to get around these three precursors by using a range of ingenious narrative tricks. If in Baldwin's earliest essays and short stories we can clearly perceive the outlines of his agon—his struggle with Stowe and Wright, his implicit idolization of James—his first novel, *Go Tell It on the Mountain,* becomes a crucial space, a literary proving ground. He struggles resourcefully to avoid the pitfalls of *Uncle Tom's Cabin* and *Native Son.* Even allowing for what is at bottom an ambivalent response, Baldwin reads the two novels consciously as literary object lessons to be studiously avoided. The primary source of his perspicacious polemics against Wright and Stowe is, as noted above, his own growing will to power as a writer. So, too, it is the source of his admiration for Henry James.

Go Tell It on the Mountain is complex but it has a simple plot. John Grimes, the stepson of a Harlem minister, Gabriel Grimes, wakes up on his fourteenth birthday and hopes someone remembers. His mother, Elizabeth, is the only person who does not forget. Part I, "The Seventh Day," is essentially a brief portrait of John, an adolescent artist embattled by his contradictory impulses for and against the religious life of his mother and stepfather; Part II, "The Prayer of the Saints," with three subsections, "Gabriel's Prayer," "Florence's Prayer," and "Elizabeth's Prayer," reveals the past lives and sins of the Reverend Gabriel Grimes, his sister Florence, and his wife Elizabeth, John's mother. Each is told from a third-person limited point of view with extended flashbacks and stream of consciousness facilitated by the ongoing church service— saintly prayers, singing, testimony, and confession. In the final section, "The Threshing Floor," we return briefly to John on the "threshing floor" of the church as presumably vast and impersonal forces battle for his soul. In a sense, "The Thresh-ing Floor" could have easily been called "John's Prayer."

In "Elizabeth's Prayer," the precursors—Stowe, Wright, James—converge. Yet Baldwin successfully negotiates his nar-rative around all three, splicing together elegant variations on their themes and techniques. If, for example, Baldwin presents Elizabeth's life to us from a Jamesian third-person limited nar-rative perspective, if he superficially characterizes her as the sort of Christian—devout and God-fearing—whom Stowe passionately celebrates in *Uncle Tom's Cabin,* he boldly super-imposes these elements upon a forceful and clearly identifiable black idiom and tradition. Elizabeth (who bears the name of the mother of John the Baptist) is transported into a kind of continuous past, a glorious, if troubled, remembrance of her life before Gabriel and before the birth of John. Even the manner in which her memories are invoked belongs to the tradition of the black church. When Elisha plays the piano, he plays a hymn the congregation has often heard, a crucial key of their lives, as of the lives of their forebears. So Elisha's musical performance allows us to observe Baldwin's authori-tative orchestration of his narrative. Baldwin contextualizes the narrative moment by invoking a powerful cultural signifier; Elisha plays for a black congregation, bringing back black memories. Baldwin employs sophisticated Jamesian third-person limited narration, as well as the flashback, the interior monologue—to achieve his unique and revelatory rendition of the black tradition. Elizabeth's prayer is her life. In the commingling of singing and weeping voices she instantly rec-ognizes the song Elisha plays. Although Baldwin never men-tions it by the title, it is the familiar hymn "Must Jesus Bear the Cross Alone?" Elizabeth recognizes when she hears:

> The consecrated cross I'll bear,
> Till death shall set me free,

And then go home, a crown to wear,
For there's a crown for me.

(*Go Tell It on the Mountain,* p. 152)

Elizabeth "had been hearing this song all her life . . . but she had never understood it as well as she understood it now. It filled the church, as though the church had merely become a hollow or a void, echoing with the voices that had driven her to this dark place."

The cross in Baldwin's fiction does not stand as an unambiguous symbol of Christian redemption. In his hands, the cross does not symbolize here, as it seems to to Stowe, a Christian vision of righteousness and purity. It is, in Baldwin's imaginative world, a dubious iconographic symbol, threatening to destroy the very life it ostensibly nurtures and protects. It becomes the symbol of compromise or perpetual adjustment to what may be a rather stunning series of personal disasters. Thus, in each saint's life the cross takes on specific meaning. For Elizabeth, it will always be connected to her love for Richard, who profoundly tests and contests her faith. When Elizabeth questions God, Baldwin moves beyond the sentimental ethos of the idealized Christianity of Stowe's *Uncle Tom's Cabin.* Even when, in brief moments, Stowe allows George Harris to wonder out loud about the existence of God and about the divine role in the perpetuation of slavery, Stowe, after the fashion of a catechism, has a ready-made answer, which asserts, in so many words, "Christ is the way, the truth, the light."

Baldwin juxtaposes the wonder of Christianity in black life with its terror, and in some cases its tyranny. The relationship between Elizabeth and Richard highlights the complex and contradictory nature of black Christianity. We have already noted Baldwin's ambivalent response to religion in "Notes of a Native Son," and he had certainly noticed, in *Black Boy,* the tyrannical religious community which Richard Wright defied.

Thus, Elizabeth's first lover, Richard, represents, in many re-spects, the vision of Richard Wright. Richard's name is surely not a random selection. Richard, like his namesake Richard Wright, outspokenly opposes the tyranny of religion in black American life. Baldwin portrays Richard in a way that is some-what like Wright's depiction of Bigger Thomas. But there are striking differences, which reflect Baldwin's compensatory nar-rative urge to negotiate around the threatening limitations of *Native Son*. Wright's imaginative failure in *Native Son*, as Bald-win sees it in "Many Thousands Gone," is his negligence of "Negro life as a continuing and complex group reality." He fails to present "that depth of involvement and unspoken rec-ognition of shared experience." In *Go Tell It on the Mountain* their respective pasts haunt the lives of Gabriel, Florence, and Elizabeth and inspire their perpetual sense of guilt, and we witness how the sins of the fathers and mothers are visited upon the sons, daughters, and lovers. Even before we know all about Richard, before we observe how he resembles or recalls Richard Wright and Bigger Thomas, we learn how deeply Richard, lover of Elizabeth and father of John, affects their lives long after his death:

Not even tonight, in the heart's nearly impenetrable secret place, where the truth is hidden and where only the truth can live, could she wish that she had not known him; or deny that, so long as he was there, the rejoicing of Heaven could have meant nothing to her—that, being forced to choose between Richard and God, she could only, even with weeping, have turned away from God.

And this was why God had taken him from her. It was for all of this that she was paying now, and it was this pride, hatred, bitterness, lust—this folly, this corruption—of which her son was heir.

(*Go Tell It on the Mountain*, pp. 157–58)

In *Native Son* Bigger Thomas has no significant emotional relationships, or, so Baldwin believes, Wright fails to reveal them. Bigger's involvement with Bessie Mears appears more or less to be an arrangement for the protagonist's sexual convenience, an arrangement that eases his anxiety, frustration, and fear. Although Baldwin takes care to show the developing relationship between Richard and Elizabeth, even so Richard reminds us of Bigger Thomas. Baldwin corroborates their similarity by connecting Richard to details that recall *Native Son*. Richard, for instance, knows and understands the music Elizabeth hears. And he, like Bigger, takes a defiant stand against it. As Baldwin exploits a moment in *Native Son,* recalling Bigger Thomas's defiant shout, "I can die without a cross," we discover that, "wild and unhappy," Richard shares a similar view. Neither Richard nor his friends—"hard drinking, hard talking" "lewd and lustful"—ever go to church. "In their speech, in their lives, and in their hearts they all cursed God. They all seemed to be saying as Richard, when she once timidly mentioned the love of Jesus, said: 'You can tell that puking bastard to kiss my big black ass.'" Richard dies without believing in the redemptive power that the cross symbolizes. Yet his death, indeed his bloody crucifixion, creates for Elizabeth a new heaven and a new earth. His painful legacy becomes her angry and avenging will to survive.

In the writer's portrayal of Richard's and Elizabeth's relationship, we can see Baldwin's agon—the dogged presence of Wright, Stowe, and James—dramatically spelling itself out. The convergence of the three powers fuels his narrative and allows him to achieve unique creative authority. When, for example, Richard refers to Jesus as a "puking bastard," one could argue, as Baldwin characterizes Bigger in "Everybody's Protest Novel," that Richard is merely "Uncle Tom's descendant, flesh of his flesh." But Richard, unlike Bigger, represents far more than "exactly opposite a portrait" of Uncle Tom. Although Richard is certainly reminiscent of Bigger, the crucial difference Baldwin takes care to reveal is Richard's capacity to love. He clearly loves Elizabeth and she loves him. He is twenty-two, a grocery clerk, and she is eighteen. When Elizabeth first meets Richard, she views him as "sullen" and "only barely polite." But when Elizabeth eventually introduces herself to him, he smiles:

"You remember that day," he asked much later, "when you came into the store?"
"Yes?"
"Well, you was mighty pretty."
"I didn't think you never looked at me."
"You was reading a book."
"Yes."
"What book was it, Richard?"
"Oh I don't remember. Just a book."

(Go Tell It on the Mountain, p. 160)

This is more Richard Wright than Bigger Thomas. They quickly get to know each other and fall in love. Each chooses, essentially for personal reasons, to leave the South. And even if Richard hates the South where as a black boy he was deeply scarred by Jim Crow laws and customs, his private dream is his primary motivation. His love for Elizabeth, and the possibility of marriage to her, suggests his genuine hope for individual fulfillment. Elizabeth negotiates her way out of her aunt's house in the South and to New York City in order to continue her relationship with him:

In those days, had the Lord Himself descended from Heaven with trumpets telling her to turn back, she could scarcely have heard Him, and could certainly not have heeded. She lived in those days, in a fiery storm, of which Richard was the center and the heart. And she fought only to reach him.

(Go Tell It on the Mountain, p. 161)

The manner in which Baldwin depicts the relationship between Elizabeth and Richard is a revealing example of how he manages to use the ambivalent triple literary legacy of Stowe, Wright, and James to achieve his own narrative authority. Richard defies the Christian way of life idealized by Stowe, and because of his defiance, Elizabeth's devotion is necessarily compromised. By presenting Richard as someone capable of love—even romantic love—Baldwin struggles to avoid portraying his characters as mere products of their environments. Richard is considerably more than "a member of a Society or a Group," as he put it in "Everybody's Protest Novel." Baldwin presents his characters' successes and failures in terms of their individual choices and personalities. The forceful consequences of Richard's and Elizabeth's relationship deeply affect the life of their illegitimate son, John, even before John's birth and long after Richard's death.

If Richard appears somewhat reminiscent of Bigger Thomas, indifferent and insolent, he also possesses other sides. He and Elizabeth are emotionally as well as intellectually engaged. In one Jamesian scene Richard and Elizabeth stroll through various museums:

And when he took her to the Museum of Natural History, or the Metropolitan Museum of Art, where they were almost certain to be the only black people, and he guided her through the halls, which never ceased in her imagination to be as cold as tombstones, it was then she saw another life in him.

For she never grasped—not at any rate with her mind—what with such incandescence, he tried to tell her on these Saturday afternoons. She could not find, between herself and the African statuette, or totem pole, on which he gazed with such melancholy wonder, any point of contact. She was only glad that she did not look that way. She preferred to look in the other museum, at the paintings; but still she did not understand anything he said about them. She did not know why he so adored things that were so long dead; what sustenance they gave him, and what secrets he hoped to wrest from them. But she understood, at least, that they *did* give him a kind of bitter nourishment, and that the secrets they held for him were a matter of his life and death.

(*Go Tell It on the Mountain*, pp. 165–66)

This scene tells us as much about Baldwin's own struggle to achieve narrative authority as it reveals about Richard and Elizabeth. There are moments in any writer's work that unexpectedly distill or clarify the quintessential nature of the writer's deepest concerns. This passage represents a metonym of Baldwin's agon. James surfaces, genielike, through the writer's portrayal of Richard, allowing Baldwin to translate or to transpose James's aesthetic theory.

Like Peter of "Previous Condition," Richard dismisses the American custom and prejudicial expectation that blacks should remain uptown in Harlem. Like Peter, he does not wish to be typecast or, like Baldwin, to allow race to stand as the primary key to his identity. But while Richard questions and tests the absurd social customs and expectations that keep other blacks out of the Metropolitan Museum of Art, Elizabeth reveals her suspicion of high culture. Like Christopher Newman of James's *The American,* she personifies America's untutored awe and deference before the grandeur of European history and culture. The museum becomes the space in which her American assumptions of self and the world will be challenged. So, also, in the opening of *The American,* Christopher Newman tours the Louvre. Unlike Elizabeth, who fails to find "any point of contact," Richard can appreciate the connection between his life and the culture that produces the African statuette or totem pole. The guided tour he provides for the woman he loves suggests self-exploration and definition. It suggests the redemptive power of Art, Art as a religion. Yet the experience in the museum is paradoxically exclusive—most people do not visit museums in glamorous cities—as well as universal.

Art possesses the extraordinary, indeed inscrutable, power to move and motivate men and women beyond the wildest dreams of its creators. With its timeless beauty and captured wisdom, Art can inspire and lead one, regardless of personal background or circumstances, to, as Baldwin puts it in "Everybody's Protest Novel," "freedom which cannot be legislated, fulfillment which cannot be charted." To be sure, the Art in museums and in the great cathedrals of Europe are products of enormous human suffering, including slavery and war, and Henry James, of course, is poignantly aware of this. But Art, nevertheless, reigns supreme and works as religion does in mysterious ways to perform its wonders. This seeming religious significance—an inherent inspiration and faith that supersedes particular moments and circumstances—is analogous to the faith Elisha's music inspires in the congregation of which Elizabeth is a devout member. Elizabeth, however, comes unprepared to receive inspiration. She represents the stranger in the village of high culture. But Baldwin has orchestrated a romantic as well as a cultural encounter. Although she cannot appreciate the art, she wonders about "the sustenance" the works of art provide to Richard as well as "the secrets" he hopes "to wrest from them." On a deeper level, she intuitively knows her man: "She understood, at least, that they [the paintings and sculptures] *did* give him a kind of bitter nourishment, and that the secrets they held for him were a matter of his life and death." Baldwin creates this other life, this other aspect of Richard's personality, to save Richard from the fate of Bigger Thomas, and his novel from what he perceives to be the limitations of *Native Son*.

Furthermore, the figure of the young black artist—eager and defiant—is hidden in the texture of the scene. Call him Richard or call him James, he perceives in Art and receives from it "a kind of bitter nourishment." It is "a matter of his life and death." Although vaguely disguised, the Wright of *Black Boy* and *American Hunger* and the Baldwin of *Notes of a Native Son* assert themselves here. Like Richard, they (Baldwin and Wright) identify simultaneously with the lonely struggle of the artist and the artist's magnificent virtuosity and triumph. In *Black Boy* Wright dreams: "I dreamed of going North and writing books, novels. The North symbolized to me all that I had not felt and seen; it had no relation whatever to

what actually existed. Yet, by imagining a place where everything was possible, I kept hope alive in me" (*Black Boy*, p. 147).
In *American Hunger* Wright says explicitly that he "managed
to keep humanly alive through transfusions from books,"
pointing out that writing "was the single aim of my living."[1]
One gets a similar sense of the mortal nature of this issue in
Baldwin's "Notes of a Native Son" when he tells his father he
would rather write than preach!

Baldwin achieves his own narrative authority even while he
repeats, translates, or transposes the scenes, themes, and characters of his literary forebears. If, for example, Richard symbolizes, in some measure, the artistic type capable of learning
"the secrets" or lessons of the masters, he must perpetually
"wrest" such information from them. This phenomenon constitutes his complex American fate. The other cultivated "life"
Elizabeth sees in him is hard won but, as Richard sees it,
utterly necessary. On one of their romantic Jamesian strolls,
Richard tells Elizabeth why he has educated himself:

> "I just decided one day that I was going to get to know everything
> them white bastards knew, and I was going to get to know it better
> than them, so could no white son-of-a-bitch *nowhere* never talk *me*
> down, and never make me feel like I was dirt, when I could read
> him the alphabet, back, front, and sideways. Shit—he weren't going
> to beat my ass, then. And if he tried to kill me, I'd take him with
> me, I swear to my mother I would."
>
> (*Go Tell It on the Mountain*, p. 167)

Richard could easily be an articulate Bigger Thomas venting
his existential rage in black street argot. But Richard's avenging
passion is born of his pride, and his love for Elizabeth, as
much as of his hate.

If we can take, at least in this instance, Robert Stepto's
insistence that the quest for freedom and literacy is a "pregeneric myth" of Afro-American literature, Richard's comments
assume even greater weight. When "the alphabet" is illumi-

nated in bold relief as the ultimate key to Afro-American self-definition and the weapon against arbitrary categorization, other black voices and texts are dramatically evoked.[2] In such traditional light, Richard's comments, at first apparently simply an angry outburst, come to reveal a greater poignancy and depth that repeats the urgent yearnings of Frederick Douglass, Harriet Jacobs, W. E. B. Du Bois, Richard Wright, Ralph Ellison, and other black writers who use language and literacy in behalf of human dignity and freedom.

If Baldwin manages to orchestrate an effective kind of counterpoint to Wright and James, there are nonetheless moments when one writer somehow manages to dominate. Richard's fate is Bigger Thomas's fate reenacted with subtle differences. Richard is driven to self-destructive rage by the whites he so passionately despises. He is crucified on the cross of white refusal to see his individual humanity. Stealing from Wright's plot, Baldwin allows Richard, like Bigger, to be caught in the wrong place at the wrong time. And recalling Wright yet again, Richard is arrested because some black boys, unlike those in the failed attempt in *Native Son,* rob a white man's store. Returning home one night after visiting Elizabeth, he stands on a subway platform. His fate is sealed as he sees three black boys being chased by two white men:

Then he came full awake; in panic, he knew that whatever the trouble was, it was now his trouble also; for these white men would make no distinction between him and the three boys they were after: They were all colored, they were about the same age, and here they stood together on the subway platform. And they were all, with no questions asked, herded upstairs, and into the wagon and to the station house.

(*Go Tell It on the Mountain,* p. 171)

Despite his attempts to define and thereby free himself through literacy, and whatever the nature of the "bitter nour-

ishment" he receives from Art, Richard becomes instanta-
neously, to use Baldwin's description of Bigger, "the incarnation of a myth." In the eyes of the wounded white man he is
another Bigger Thomas.

"You black bastards," the man said, looking at him, "you're all the
same." And Richard said, but quietly, knowing that he was lost:
"But all the same, mister, I wasn't there." And he looked at the white
man's bloody shirt and thought, he told Elizabeth, at the bottom of
his heart: "I wish to God they'd killed you."
                              (*Go Tell It on the Mountain*, pp. 171–72)

The episode of the subway chase converges in specific ways
with Wright's *Native Son* and then diverges toward the aesthetics of James. Bigger Thomas and his friends scheme to rob
a white man's store. Bigger emerges larger than life in all the
Chicago newspapers as a psychopathic rapist and murderer,
yet he cannot bring himself to rob a white man. He is gripped
by deep-seated incapacitating fear. Furthermore, Bigger and
his cronies dream of opportunities out of reach because they
are black. As a plane soars high above them, they—unemployed, uneducated, ill-housed, and ill-clothed—dream mo-
mentarily of flying like the white boys. Of course, they quickly
remind each other, bitterly, that they will never fly because
blacks cannot attend aviation school. So, too, Baldwin's scene
is a slice of urban life—the racial hierarchy, the blind white
prejudice, the bitter black resentment and hate. But his scene
has a Jamesian component; Richard experiences a moment of
revelation that leads to his death. It is a moment highly reminiscent of Jamesian self-discovery, an ironic perception of
one's life situation. Richard recognizes his peculiar and complex American fate. He understands that he will, repeatedly,
be mistaken for someone he is not. He will be gratuitously
victimized by the failure of others to see him. Richard is eventually acquitted and freed, but he kills himself shortly there-

after, slashing his wrists with his razor. His landlady finds him the next morning "dead among the scarlet sheets." Even Elizabeth's love cannot save him.

But why should Richard kill himself so abruptly? What in the novel prepares us for his suicide? This apparent first novelist's blunder toward facile resolution and quick narrative fix hardly appears Jamesian. But it is conceivable that Baldwin has in mind Roderick Hudson, one of James's earliest characters, who, torn between his study of law and his love of sculpture, becomes ensnarled in a hopeless love triangle, loses his artistic inspiration, and falls to his death during a mountain walk.

In both "Notes of a Native Son" and "Previous Condition" Baldwin demonstrates the venomous effects of black rage and resentment. In "Previous Condition" Peter, like Richard, dares to be different. But after a while he becomes overwhelmed by his bitter resentment. He tells his friend Jules, "'I'm not Booker T. Washington. . . . I want to emancipate myself. If this goes on much longer . . . I'll blow my top, I'll break somebody's head.'" The combination of rage and corrosive self-doubt becomes overwhelming. Richard's suicide represents a violent and tragic enactment of such racial resignation. Whether Richard's suicide strikes one as probable or implausible, Baldwin emphatically highlights the consequences and implications of Richard's death. Before Richard's suicide, Elizabeth discovers that she is pregnant with his child. She lacks the courage to tell him as she had planned to do the night before he killed himself—she didn't because she felt it might seem just another burden. Ironically, Richard's sense of himself as a potential father might have inspired a measure of optimism and saved his life.

Richard's situation before his suicide deeply affected Elizabeth in other ways. While Richard was in jail, Elizabeth had begun to hate whites. Not long before he died, "She looked out into the quiet streets, and for the first time in her life, she hated it all—the white city, the white world." Baldwin continues:

She could not, that day, think of one decent white person in the whole world. She sat there, and she hoped that one day God, with tortures inconceivable, would grind them utterly into humility, and make them know that black boys and black girls, whom they treated with such condescension, such disdain, and such good humor, had hearts like human beings, too, more human hearts than theirs.

(*Go Tell It on the Mountain*, p. 173)

The language and imagery of this passage echoes and reflects Wright's *Native Son*. Elizabeth's bitterness and hatred is Bigger Thomas's. There is a similar description in *Native Son*:

To Bigger and his kind white people were not really people; they were a sort of great natural force, like a stormy sky looming overhead, or like a deep swirling river stretching suddenly at one's feet in the dark. As long as he and his black folks did not go beyond certain limits, there was no need to fear that white force. But whether they feared it or not, each and every day of their lives they lived with it; even when words did not sound its name, they acknowledged its reality. As long as they lived here in this prescribed corner of the city, they paid mute tribute to it.

(*Native Son*, p. 109)

Bigger is responding to the vast, impersonal nature of "the white force." Elizabeth's own hatred, of "the white city, the white world," has been inspired by and deeply affected by her love for Richard. Wright asserts that "the white force" is always already present—"each and every day of their lives they lived with it; even when words did not sound its name, they acknowledged its reality"; Baldwin demonstrates how racial prejudice invades and corrupts private relationships. This turn of the narrative screw, an intense focusing on relationships, confirms Baldwin's indebtedness to James.

By exploiting the aesthetic legacies of both Wright and James, Baldwin renders what is arguably the most complex and revealing portrait of a black youth in the history of American fiction. Baldwin's remarkable characterization of John demonstrates how the lives of the young protagonist's fore-bears deeply influence his own. One of Baldwin's principal artistic aims here is to show the complex web of associations and relationships of Afro-American life, a portrayal he found lacking in Wright's *Native Son,* but a complex web like that fully depicted in, say, James's *The Ambassadors.*

After Richard's death, Elizabeth seriously begins to question her ability to nurture and protect their son:

What questions would he ask her, what answers would she give? She surely would not be able to lie to him indefinitely about his father. . . . And she thought of the boys who had gone to prison. . . . Would John be one of these boys one day? How could she hope, alone, and in famine, as she was, to put herself between him and this so wide and raging destruction?

(*Go Tell It on the Mountain,* p. 178)

Her loneliness and insecurity eventually lead her to Gabriel, a Pentecostal minister. They marry, and Gabriel promises Elizabeth, and swears before God, that he will love John "just like he was my own." But he reneges, incapable of loving John. He feels guilty because Royal, the apple of his eye, son of an earlier marriage in the South, is dead, and as a consequence resents John as a constant reminder of his own past failures as well as a living symbol of Elizabeth's fall from the glory of God.

The technical ingenuity of "Elizabeth's Prayer," as of "Florence's Prayer" and "Gabriel's Prayer," allows Baldwin to make numerous revelations about the characters' past lives that might have proved tedious in a different narrative form. His contextualization of these revelatory prayers demonstrates unique grace and power. Gabriel and Florence, his sister, the only person who can stand up against Gabriel, are major players in this fervent and enduring night of black testimony and remembering. Baldwin's narrative trick, his intense focus on relationships, in a sense stolen from James, becomes his unique handiwork because he makes it culturally specific.[3] In the first section of the book, which prepares the reader for the revelations in "Elizabeth's Prayer," we see John first in relation to the Reverend Gabriel Grimes, the only father he knows—his stepfather. Baldwin lets us know that a principal theme of *Go Tell It on the Mountain* will be paternal priority—the inescapable consequences of a father's life working themselves out in the life of a son: "Everyone had always said that John would be a preacher when he grew up, just like his father. It had been said so often that John, without ever thinking about it, had come to believe it himself." We discover that John and Gabriel are engaged in something reminiscent of an Oedipal struggle. Gabriel, at least by the time John knows him as his father, has been born again and has moved beyond the folly and sordid sins of his youth. He, as a preacher and father, is a stern disciplinarian. John has an inchoate artistic sensibility and, like James Joyce's Stephen Daedalus and Thomas Mann's Tonio Kröger, he yearns to experience the bliss of the commonplace, though his precocious power of perception and intelligence distinguishes him among his peers.

When the children in John's class are asked to write the alphabet on the blackboard and the principal points to John's letters and asks, "Which child is that?", John suspects punishment, but the principal says, "You're a very bright boy, John Grimes . . . keep up the good work." Her praise leaves John in the shock of profound recognition: "That moment gave him, from that time on, if not a weapon at least a shield; he apprehended totally, without belief or understanding, that he had in himself a power that other people lacked; that he could use this to save himself, to raise himself; and that, perhaps, with this power he might one day win that love which he so longed for." Even before the reader's awareness of Richard and his hard won literacy, Baldwin has deftly foreshadowed his passionate speech to Elizabeth: "'I just decided one day that I was going to get to know everything them white bastards knew, and I was going to get to know it better than them, so could no white son-of-a-bitch *nowhere* never talk *me* down, and never make me feel like dirt, when I could read him the alphabet, back, front, and sideways.'" John will not, like Bigger Thomas, become "the incarnation of a myth" or a "symbolic monster."

This initial sense of John prepares us for the deep revelations about him that eventually come in "Elizabeth's Prayer," where we discover the very circumstances during which he was literally conceived. Consequently, the question of his extraordinary intelligence and his intuitive rebellion, his yearning for his "individual existence," is answered when we come to know his biological father. Intelligence and defiance are in his blood. John's life is deeply affected by forces beyond the Reverend Grimes's religious power and paternal scorn. He does not know how his dead biological father affects him, but Baldwin makes sure that the reader does. When, in the opening section of the novel, only his mother remembers his birthday, John uses her gift to go downtown to a movie on 42nd Street. He knows his stepfather will strongly disapprove, but he is goaded defiantly on by an enigmatic force: "*Broadway*! the way that led to death was broad . . . but narrow was the way that led to life eternal. . . . In the narrow way, the way of the cross, there awaited him only humiliation forever; there awaited him one day a house like his father's house, and a church like his father's and a job like his father's." John identifies with the most defiant character in the movie he saw: "She walked the cold, foggy streets, a little woman and not pretty, with a lewd, brutal swagger, saying to the whole world: 'You can kiss my ass.' . . . She never thought of prayer." Another extraordinary foreshadowing, for we later discover Richard's response to

Elizabeth's belief in the love of Jesus: "'You can tell that puking bastard to kiss my big black ass.'"

When we move out of "Elizabeth's Prayer" into "The Threshing Floor," John, for the duration of a night, is in a religious trance. John hears the voice of the Holy Ghost saying in several ways "Jesus Saves," but an "ironic voice," surely Richard's, "insisted yet once more that he rise from that filthy floor if he did not want to become like all the other niggers." As this dramatic battle for John's soul plays itself out, John hears the ironic voice again, in a mocking reply to the Reverend Gabriel Grimes: "'Set thine house in order,' said his father, 'for thou shalt die and not live.' And then the ironic voice spoke again saying: 'Get up, John. Get up, boy. Don't let him keep you here. You got everything your daddy got.'"

If there is any doubt about the source of the ironic voice, John at one point envisions a grave, and later, when the focus is on Elizabeth, she remembers her first conversation with Richard: "'You remember that day when you came into the store.' 'I didn't think you never looked at me.'"

In the end, and whatever the consequences of John's night on the "threshing floor," his life will represent a varied confluence of powerful forces. His fate, like Baldwin's, will necessarily be complex, as complex as the music he hears throughout the novel:

This sound had filled John's life, so it now seemed, from the moment he had first drawn breath. He had heard it everywhere, in prayer and in daily speech, and wherever the saints were gathered, and in the unbelieving streets. It was in his father's anger, and in his mother's calm insistence, and in the vehement mockery of his aunt; it had rung, so oddly, in Roy's voice this afternoon, and when Elisha played the piano it was there; it was in the beat and jangle of Sister McCandless's tambourine, it was in the very cadence of her testimony, and invested that testimony with a matchless, unimpeachable authority. Yes, he had heard it all his life, but it was only now that his ears were opened to this sound that came from darkness, that could only come from darkness, that yet bore such sure witness to the glory of the light.

(Go Tell It on the Mountain, p. 200)

The "matchless, unimpeachable authority" John hears is the sound of the souls of black folk. Thus, even as Baldwin attempts to allow John to achieve, if in "wild uneasiness," his "individual existence," the complex fate of the group the sound represents frustrates his individual will. This inescapable web of literary and historical circumstances forces Baldwin to recall "Fate," the final section of Wright's *Native Son,* his cogent criticism in "Many Thousands Gone" notwithstanding.

Wright literally and figuratively haunts the closing section of *Go Tell It on the Mountain.* Like "Fate," "The Threshing Floor" is the third and final section of Baldwin's novel. In "Fate" Wright employs a death and rebirth symbolism. Bigger refuses to eat, drink, or smoke: "There was no day for him now, and there was no night; there was but a long stretch of time" (*Native Son,* p. 254). Bigger experiences a similar moment to the sound that issues forth and echoes through John's darkness. He listens to the preacher who comes to visit him in his cell. And for the duration of this heightened and sustained recollection, the preacher, even in Bigger's life, achieves, in Baldwin's words, "a matchless, unimpeachable authority." The sound and the cadence of the preacher's words transport Bigger to deeper and nearly inaccessible regions of himself:

If someone had afterwards asked him to repeat the preacher's words, he would not have been able to do so. But he felt and sensed their meaning. As the preacher talked there appeared before him a vast black silent void and the images of the preacher swam in that void, grew large and powerful; familiar images which his mother had given him when he was a child at her knee; images which in turn aroused impulses long dormant, impulses that he had suppressed and sought to shunt from his life. They were images which had once given him a reason for living, had explained the world. Now they sprawled before his eyes and seized his emotions in a spell of awe and wonder. . . . an endless reach of deep murmuring waters upon whose face was darkness and there was no form no shape no sun no stars and no land and a voice came out of the darkness and the waters moved to obey and there emerged slowly a huge spinning ball and the voice said *let there be light* and there was light.

(Native Son, p. 263)

There are two rather significant connections in this passage. As the sermon continues, Wright plays back to us through the dark stream of Bigger's consciousness James Weldon Johnson's "The Creation." The sound and imagery effectively return to us, as to Bigger, with a kind of alienated and incandescent majesty: ". . . and with thundering rustling the waters drained off and the mountain peaks reared into view and there were valleys and rivers and the voice called the dry land *earth* and the waters *seas* and the earth grew grass and trees and flowers that gave off seed that fell to the earth to grow again and the earth was lit by the light of a million stars." Also, the beginning of this passage is highly reminiscent of the moment in *Notes of a Native Son* when Baldwin hears at his father's funeral one of his father's favorite songs and is taken back by its familiar strains to his childhood days. He remembers the joy, beauty, and genuine paternal pride, which in his adolescent "rage" he had long since forgotten. But if John is deeply haunted by his dead father, Richard, Baldwin as writer finds himself in a similar situation, haunted by his own literary father, the other Richard; it is his complex and ambivalent literary fate to recall Wright's *Native Son* here:

Then the darkness began to murmur—a terrible sound—and John's ear trembled. . . . And now in his moaning, and so far from any help, he heard it in himself. . . . It was a sound of rage and weeping which filled the grave, rage and weeping from time set free, but bound now in eternity; rage that had no language, weeping with no voice—which yet spoke now, to John's startled soul, of boundless melancholy, of the bitterest patience, and the longest night; of the deepest water, the strongest chains, the most cruel lash; of humility most wretched, the dungeon most absolute, of love's bed defiled, and birth dishonored, and most bloody unspeakable, sudden death. Yes, the darkness hummed with murder, the body in the water, the body in the fire, the body in the tree. John looked down the line of these avenues of darkness, army upon army, and his soul whispered: *Who are these? Who are they? And wondered where shall I go?*

(*Go Tell It on the Mountain*, p. 201)

Baldwin did not, of course, wish to be known as "*merely* a Negro; or, even, merely a Negro writer*," yet in borrowing Wright's imagery of murmuring water and darkness, he spells out a similar metonymic creation of the Afro-American world. He refers repeatedly to the "rage" which, like Bigger's hate, is "rage that had no language." We are reminded of the "bitterest patience" of black slaves who wore "the strongest chains" and received "the most cruel lash." Still, this passage suggests more than the violence of the slaveholder's world and it moves even beyond the short and brutal lives of so many native sons. At 4605 Drexel Boulevard, the Dalton mansion, we recall the eerie red glow of the fiery furnace in Wright's magnificent decapitation scene, when John thinks, "Yes, the darkness hummed with murder . . . the body in the fire." Later, after John has risen from the threshing floor and is walking home, "A lean cat stalked the gutter and fled as they approached; turned to watch them, with yellow, malevolent eyes, from the ambush of a garbage can." Similarly, the Daltons' white cat perches on Mary Dalton's trunk and observes the decapitation scene through two "green burning pools, pools of accusation and guilt" (*Native Son*, p. 90).

This moving variation and repetition of *Native Son*'s theme, inspired by the sound which "had filled John's life . . . from the moment he had drawn breath" takes us back to "Elizabeth's Prayer," which becomes, in Baldwin's deft hands, the repository, the record of the tragicomic sound and significance of the Afro-American soul. We witness what Du Bois called, at the beginning of the century, "the peculiar sensation" of Afro-America's "double consciousness"—"two souls, two thoughts, two unreconciled strivings, in one dark body whose dogged strength alone keeps it from being torn asunder."[4] From this perspective, "the consecrated cross" Elizabeth must necessarily bear, as the song reminds her, "till death shall set me free" symbolizes the irony of the Afro-American presence in American life. Issuing forth in religious and musical splendor, that cross represents the iconographic power of Mount Calvary. It speaks for the many thousands gone. The cross has been consecrated by anonymous black blood. It reminds us how the American version of the idealized Christian vision is perpetually mocked by the sins of the Founding Fathers and the sons. For it set in motion, as Ralph Ellison has so eloquently pointed out, assumptions by which Afro-Americans, through legislation and custom, would perpetually stand in America's collective psyche as the crucified victim, the scapegoat, of both the failure and promise of democracy.[5] In light of the Afro-American's paradoxical situation, Baldwin understands what Henry James means when James describes being an American as an "arduous task."

V "OUT OF DISORDER, THE ORDER WHICH IS ART"

James Baldwin and the "Mighty" Henry James

These were the things the most inspiring, in the sense that while generations, while worlds had come and gone, they seemed far most to prevail and survive and testify. As he stood before them the perfection of their survival often struck him as the supreme eloquence, the virtue that included all others, thanks to the universal language of art, the richest and most universal. Empires and systems and conquests had rolled over the globe and every kind of greatness had risen and passed away, but the beauty of the great pictures had known nothing of death or change, and the tragic centuries had only sweetened their freshness. The same faces, the same figures looked out at different worlds, knowing so many secrets the particular world didn't, and when they joined hands they made the indestructible thread on which the pearls of history were strung.

—Henry James, *The Tragic Muse*

In "As Much Truth as One Can Bear," an article that appeared in the *New York Times Book Review* on January 14, 1962, Baldwin criticizes Ernest Hemingway, F. Scott Fitzgerald, John Dos Passos, and William Faulkner for a failure to see the world from a cosmopolitan perspective. While maintaining that he has "genuine respect" for their achievements, he takes issue with them for exemplifying "the American way of looking on the world, as a place to be corrected, and in which innocence is inexplicably lost."[1]

He calls Henry James, in contrast, "the greatest of our novelists." He bases his judgment on, among other achievements, James's characterization of Lambert Strether in *The Ambassadors*:

What is the moral dilemma of Lambert Strether if not that, at the midnight hour, he realizes that he has, somehow inexplicably, failed his manhood . . . the responsibility that men must take upon themselves of facing and reordering reality.

Strether's triumph is that he is able to realize this, even though he knows it is too late for him to act on it. And it is James' perception of this peculiar impossibility which makes him, until today, the greatest of our novelists. For the question which he raised . . . is the question which so torments us now . . . How is an American to become a man? And this is precisely the same thing as asking: How is America to become a nation? By contrast with him, the giants who came to the fore between the two World Wars merely lamented the necessity.[2]

Baldwin's interpretation of Strether's dilemma as indicative of James's singular achievement as a writer also suggests a grand American project yet to be fulfilled. Baldwin's reading of *The Ambassadors* allows him to take up the arduous task where James left it. By translating Strether's "moral dilemma" into a national issue, Baldwin can justify his own exploration of America's racial and sexual attitudes. These recurrent themes in his work give him a kind of authority beyond James. Why, then, does Baldwin, a black writer inevitably concerned with his social as well as literary situation in American society, choose James as "our greatest novelist"?

Baldwin's promotion of Henry James to the highest rank, we could argue, derives as much from James's experiments with points of view or a "central intelligence" in his work as from the "alienated" way in which James explores the discovery of what it means to be an American. Baldwin believes that Wright and Stowe clearly fall short of the true aims of the artist, although both *Native Son* and *Uncle Tom's Cabin* deeply influenced him. But he also specifically listed James's *The Portrait of a Lady* and *The Princess Casamassima* as two of the ten novels that aided him in his "break out of the ghetto."[3] Later, in a 1984 *Paris Review* interview, Baldwin gives James the credit for having helped him solve technical aspects of *Go Tell It on the Mountain* (1953) "after ten years of carrying the book around."

The book was very hard to write because I was too young when I started, seventeen. . . . There were things I couldn't deal with technically at first. . . . This is where reading Henry James helped me, with his whole idea about the center of consciousness and using a single intelligence to tell the story. He gave me the idea to make the novel happen on John's birthday.[4]

If we ponder which of James's works Baldwin relies upon in arriving at his early sense of James's aesthetic theory we may safely conjecture that he refers to the prefaces to *The Portrait of a Lady* and *The Princess Casamassima*. And since he had been struggling for so long with the technical problems of his own novel, he must have taken note especially of James's extended discussion of point of view in the *Princess Casamassima* preface, his crucial distinction, for example, between "application" and "appreciation."⁵ And James's metaphor of the house of fiction in the *Portrait of a Lady* preface must have held an extraordinary appeal for an aspiring writer who had left his own house in the Harlem ghetto. James's description of the house of fiction is simultaneously democratic and exclusive. Any individual with the talent for admission necessarily chooses an individual window on the world:

The house of fiction has in short not one window but a million . . . every one of which has been pierced, or is still pierceable, in its vast front, by the need of the individual vision and by the pressure of the individual will. . . . He and his neighbors are watching the same show, but one seeing more where the other sees less, one seeing black where the other sees white.⁶

James also serves as Baldwin's example of an American writer who succeeds internationally, and one who has a long and prolific career. The manner in which James lived suggests to Baldwin a personally attractive ideal.

Baldwin must certainly have thought about his own flight in 1948 from New York to Paris (with a one-way ticket and forty-eight dollars) in relation both to Wright and James. All three of them were, for a time, expatriates by choice. Wright, in bitter, if justifiable, resentment, chose to return to the United States from Paris only for brief professional engagements. James, excluding his final judgment on America as a permanent home for himself, was nonetheless a true cosmopolitan. He zigzagged throughout Europe and across the United States, deeply engaged as an upper-class social participant yet studiously detached as an observer of both the European and the American scenes. His was always an aesthetic "adventure." James, unlike Wright, also avoided the traditional roles of husband, father, or employee, as did Baldwin. Despite striking differences, Baldwin's personal life and literary career consistently mirror James's. He, too, traveled and lived throughout the United States and Europe. He was one of the more eloquent participants in and yet detached observers of the American political and literary scene. He did not marry and he had no children. But, like James, he produced numerous books, twenty-two for Baldwin—including novels, short stories, essays, and autobiography. Dabbling, like James, with the drama, he published two plays—*The Amen Corner* (1968) and *Blues for Mr. Charlie* (1964).[7]

Examining these apparent similarities on a deeper level, we witness Baldwin's attempting to match what, in James's case, appears to have been an extraordinary personal resolution between the conflicting demands of Art and life. Most artists recognize this dualism, but in James's case it seems less of an agony than in writers of comparable discipline and talent. Because James burned his letters, and although his notebooks repeatedly reveal his creative distress over the difficulties of execution, we do not see the excruciatingly dichotomous agony that appears in the letters of, say, Gustave Flaubert to Louise Colet. It is as though James has managed, almost by instinct, to isolate the artist in himself from the man, the social creature who walks, breathes, and interacts with others. He realizes, of course, that the two "personalities" are not wholly independent. But he seeks detachment because, as James views it, creativity demands it; without it there is no clarity of vision. In other ways, the man, the social creature, can go on living a perfectly "normal" life.

Baldwin embraces and attempts, in his art and in his life, to appropriate James's theory and even some of his specific themes. He seems, at the beginning of his career, particularly preoccupied with the ideal of artistic detachment in order to achieve a transcendent coherence and beauty. We hear frequent echoes of James in his comments on the role of the American writer and of the role of writers in general. Baldwin believes that most writers view life somehow as a conspiracy against the cultivation of their talent. He seems to have James's essay "The Art of Fiction" in mind when he declares, in "Autobiographical Notes," his preface to *Notes of a Native Son*: "One writes out of one thing only—one's own experience. Everything depends on how relentlessly one forces from this experience the last drop, sweet or bitter, it can possibly give. This is the only real concern of the artist, to recreate out of the disorder of life that order which is art."[8] Baldwin has a specific conception of what life means for the artist. He concludes, in the same brief essay, that "social affairs are not generally speaking the writer's prime concern, whether they ought to be or not; it is absolutely necessary that he establish between himself and these affairs distance which will allow, at least, for clarity."

Baldwin's continual struggle to achieve the distance that will provide clarity, to live and write in accordance with a Jamesian sense of the ideal of detachment, comes across forcefully in "Princes and Powers," his reflection on Le Congrès des Ecrivains et Artistes Noirs, which was held in Paris in 1956. His dispassionate style of self-presentation is most striking and perhaps revelatory in "Princes and Powers," published in 1961 in *Nobody Knows My Name*. Because of that tone, we cannot be certain whether he thinks such a conference of black writers and artists is of any value at all. He does not appear to have been an active participant in the conference, presenting himself instead as a rather disinterested, though attentive, observer, a free-lance writer with a reporter's stance of objectivity. When Baldwin, for example, hears Léopold Senghor compare traditional European views with traditional African conceptions of art and the role of the artist, he pulls back from even the more attractive features of African aesthetics, considering them wholly inappropriate for himself and the Afro-American situation.

Baldwin is attracted to what Senghor sees as uniquely African in the creation of art. As Baldwin reports it in *Nobody Knows My Name,* "African art is concerned with reaching beyond and beneath nature, to contact, and itself become a part of, *la force vitale.* The artistic image itself is not intended to represent the thing itself, but rather the reality of the force the thing contains." Baldwin considers Senghor's characterization of African aesthetics—"the idea that the work of art expresses, contains, and is itself a part of that energy which is life," particularly appealing. Nevertheless, he suggests that nothing in Western life approximates that creative interdependence of which Senghor speaks, except "the atmosphere created among jazz musicians and their fans during a jam session." Other important differences exist. In Africa, art "is done by all, for all." When Senghor explains the congruity and simultaneity of feeling and perception in traditional African culture: "'*Sentir c'est apercevoir.*'" Baldwin observes that the division between art and life in the traditional European sense is nonexistent in African society. In contrast, "poems and stories of Europeans and Americans," according to Baldwin, "no more insisted on the actual presence of other human beings than they demanded the collaboration of a dancer and a drum." Baldwin does not think that, at this time, "social art" has significant meaning in Western life, let alone in his own. He contrasts this with Senghor, who "was speaking out of his past, where art was naturally and spontaneously social, where artistic creation did not presuppose divorce."

Baldwin goes on to celebrate the artist and the writer as loner and maverick, as a "singular intelligence" "who steals the fire."

Senghor's culture . . . did not seem to need the lonely activity of the singular intelligence on which the cultural life—the moral life—of the West depends. And a really cohesive society, one of the attributes, perhaps, of what is taken to be a "healthy" culture, has, generally, and I suspect, necessarily, a much lower level of tolerance for the maverick, the dissenter, the man who steals the fire, than have societies in which, the common ground of belief having all but vanished, each man, in awful and brutal isolation, is for himself, to flower or to perish. Or, not impossibly, to make real and fruitful again that vanished common ground, which, as I take it, is nothing more or less than the culture itself, endangered and rendered nearly inaccessible by the complexities it has, itself, inevitably created.

(Nobody Knows My Name, pp. 26–27)

Baldwin's reflection on the respective demands faced by Western and African artists displays his characteristic deep-seated ambivalence. Most of his comments on art and artists during this period, as do his fictional portrayals of artists, betray his creative dilemma. On the one hand, he wishes to be the writer as "maverick" or dissenter. But as quickly as he removes the artist from society and social affairs, he brings him back full of redemptive power. Thus, he characterizes the artist as a promethean figure who steals the fire—not for himself or Art's own sake, but for the benefit of all, the commonweal. We can see Baldwin moving toward *The Fire Next Time* of 1963, wherein he speaks in prophetic and oracular tones about the "endangered" nation. But in *The Fire Next Time,* as we have seen, the dispassionate persona of "Princes and Powers" has vanished. Baldwin is wholly engaged. He has come home to his nightmares, as did Peter in "Previous Condition" and the anonymous artist of "This Morning, This Evening, So Soon," and as he did as a boy when he came home to Harlem for his father's funeral and the riot in the streets. American "social affairs" had become fully and unequivocally the source, the subject, and the raison d'être of his singular literary intelligence. Indeed, in passages like the preceding from *Nobody*

Knows My Name: More Notes of a Native Son, even when he ostensibly rejects the social role of the writer, he invariably manages to suggest that very possibility—even the necessity of somehow making, as he puts it, "real and fruitful again that vanished common ground."

If James and Baldwin look through their special windows in the house of fiction, if one sees black where the other sees white, each has a similarly expansive view. The house in which they reside, at least during pivotal periods in their respective careers, is in the City of Light. Consequently, given their experiences as Americans abroad, both James and Baldwin seem keenly aware that Americans when removed from their native land behave even more dramatically like their fellow citizens at home. This is the theme of James's *The American.*[9] The degree to which James's novel is characteristically American is, despite its assertive title, of course, debatable. But, whatever other matters James intends to elucidate, his theme in the story of Christopher Newman, his protagonist, finding his way about Paris, is the theme of a compatriot suffering "at the hands" of a "superior civilization."

The American, James's third novel, was written at a pivotal time in his development as a writer. He had left New York for Paris just before he began to compose the novel. He hoped that it would be a commercial as well as a critical success. William Spengemann cogently points out how *The American* would have a symbolic as well as thematic significance for the remainder of James's prolific career: "At each major stage of that increasingly lonely career, Newman's story would reappear in a guise appropriate to the occasion."[10] In some profound way the peculiarly American fate of Christopher Newman becomes inextricably linked to what Baldwin calls Lambert Strether's "triumph," Strether's belated apprehension of his failure.

Baldwin's second novel, *Giovanni's Room,* is, in a sense, his

version of James's *The American*.[11] Critics have failed to understand the significance of *Giovanni's Room*'s relationship to his
literary development. Most critics concur with Robert Bone's
assessment, considering the novel little more than a quixotic
excursion onto foreign and, perhaps, forbidden territory.[12]
Failing to perceive or grant even Baldwin's stylistic accom-
plishment, Bone concludes, "*Giovanni's Room* (1956) is by far
the weakest of Baldwin's novels. There is a tentative unfinished
quality about the book, as if merely broaching the subject of
homosexuality, Baldwin has exhausted his creative energy. . . .
The characters are vague and disembodied, the themes half-
digested, we recognize from this sterile psychic landscape the
unprocessed raw material of art."[13] Baldwin received unsoli-
cited advice on his choice of subject from several book review-
ers, typical among them, Anthony West, who wrote in *The
New Yorker*, "It is to be hoped that Mr. Baldwin, a gifted writer,
will soon return to the American subjects he dealt with so
promisingly and with so much real understanding in his novel
Go Tell It on the Mountain and his brilliant collection of essays
Notes of a Native Son."[14]

But *Giovanni's Room* is as significant among Baldwin's works
as it is in Afro-American literature in general. And we can
certainly argue that if *The American* reasserts itself throughout
James's career, so *Giovanni's Room* has played a similar part in
the complex continuing drama of Baldwin's life and work. Like
James, Baldwin wrote *Giovanni's Room* at a pivotal moment in
his literary career, and, like James during the period while he
wrote *The American,* Baldwin was living in Paris and struggling with what it means to be an American. Some may argue
that, given Baldwin's racial identity, the comparison necessarily stops there. And in significant ways it obviously does.
James, to provide one salient example, could contemplate his
freedom and potential achievement, or lack of it, as an American—not as a black American. However, *Giovanni's Room* ap-

pears to swerve from the immediate and socially charged issue of race to another kind of alienation. In the story, a young American abroad struggles with his sexuality—his homosexuality—in a way that brands him, just as Christopher Newman's struggle to marry Madame de Cintré typecasts him.[15]

But while Baldwin's novel, even with a thematic twist, moves him significantly closer to James's recurrent exploration of the international theme, it distances him on the surface from his immediate ethnic precursor, Richard Wright. True, Wright himself was, ironically, also an expatriate living at that time in Paris; his *Native Son* and *Black Boy* had both become critical and commercial successes. He was regarded as the "greatest" Negro writer America had produced. Even on the thematic level, therefore, *Giovanni's Room* ostensibly represents Baldwin's powerful and conscious literary assertion of independence from Wright. It is as though Baldwin were striving to fulfill in actuality the promises of the literary manifesto he had written when criticizing both Stowe's *Uncle Tom's Cabin* and Wright's *Native Son,* and the entire tradition of the protest novel in America.

However close Baldwin comes to James, he nonetheless, as a black American writer, at least moves into uncharted thematic and cultural territory. He strives to disprove one of the suggestions James set forth in "The Future of the Novel," that the Anglo-American novel is essentially too shy to embrace fully adult life, what James describes as "the great relation between men and women, the constant world renewal."[16] Writing during the fifties, Baldwin is sufficiently courageous to write about sex and sexuality, and even bolder to write about homosexuality.

At the beginning of the story, the significant action of *Giovanni's Room* has already occurred and David painfully remembers it. Although none of Baldwin's characters are black Americans, race will be a subliminal theme. Two are white

Americans and the rest are Europeans, including Giovanni, David's lover, an "insolent and dark" Italian. In our guided tour of Parisian night life, as the plot unfolds, we find David, a young, blond American, and Giovanni hopelessly entangled *mano a mano* in each other's life. They had met after David's American girlfriend had gone to Spain as they pondered whether to become engaged. *Giovanni's Room*, on its surface at least, is a story of homosexual love. Guillaume, an aging homosexual who owns the bar in which Giovanni works, is murdered, and Giovanni is indicted for the murder; David is left saturated with guilt—bearing the burden of his desertion of Giovanni at a time of financial and emotional need.

James in *The American* and Baldwin in *Giovanni's Room* quickly establish their protagonists as American types. In his preface to *The American*, James describes the source of his inspiration:

I found myself, of a sudden, considering with enthusiasm, as the theme of a "story," the situation, in another country and an aristocratic society, of some robust but insidiously beguiled and betrayed, some cruelly wronged, compatriot: the point being in especial that he should suffer at the hands of persons pretending to represent the highest possible civilization and to be of an order in every way superior to his own. What would he "do" in that predicament, how would he right himself, or how, failing a remedy, would he conduct himself under his wrong? . . . He would let them go . . . and he would obey, in so doing, one of the large and easy impulses *generally* characteristic of his type. . . . All he would have at the end would be therefore just the moral convenience, indeed the moral necessity, of his practical, but unappreciated, magnanimity.[17]

In *Giovanni's Room*, Baldwin appropriates the same thematic formula. Each novelist situates his American character at the beginning of his respective novel. Christopher Newman is touring the Louvre and has achieved an "aesthetic headache." His gazing at Raphaels, Titians, and Rubenses inspires an unprecedented form of "self mistrust." By placing David in

Paris and testing his sense of self, sexuality, and love, Baldwin intends to reveal something about the "impulses *generally* characteristic of his type." As David describes himself in the opening paragraph as he watches his reflection in a window-pane:

My reflection is tall, perhaps rather like an arrow, my blond hair gleams. My face is like a face you have seen many times. My ancestors conquered a continent, pushing across death-laden plains, until they came to an ocean which faded away from Europe into a darker past.

(*Giovanni's Room*, p. 3)

As Baldwin and James add color and dimension to their respective portraits of their American protagonists, they take care to highlight a culturally specific background. It is, in fact, the background of each character that lands him in Paris in the first place. Christopher Newman, whose singular goal in life has been to make money, succeeds: "He had won at last and carried off his winnings; and now what was he to do with them?" The confidence "his winnings" inspires leads him to Paris. On a business trip to New York—one motivated by a desire for revenge against a fellow businessman who had wronged him—Newman decides that he has had enough of the business world. As he sits in a carriage on Wall Street, he has what is tantamount to a visionary experience:

What I wanted to get out of was Wall Street. I told the man to drive down to the Brooklyn ferry and to cross over. When we were over, I told him to drive me out into the country. . . . I spent the morning looking at the first green leaves on Long Island. I was sick of business. I wanted to throw it all up and break off short; I had money enough, or if I hadn't I ought to have; I seemed to feel a new man inside my old skin, and I longed for a new world. . . . As soon as I could get out of the game I sailed for Europe.

(*The American*, p. 57)

Thus, motivated by a disgust with the American life he knew and the type of person he had become, Newman undertakes a voyage characterized by a need for a discovery of self previously denied by geography and fate. He seeks "a new world" in the "old world." But just as his refusal to carry out his act of revenge against the businessman who had wronged him foreshadows his good-natured American nobility at the novel's end, his aims for himself when he arrives in Europe unwittingly reveal another aspect of his American innocence. He tells Tristram, another American in Paris, "I want the biggest kind of entertainment a man can get. People, places, art, nature, everything. I want to see the tallest mountains and the bluest lakes, and the finest pictures, and the handsomest churches, and the most celebrated men, and the most beautiful women."

David, too, grows to abhor his life in America. He tells us why (like Newman) he decides to leave:

What happened was that, all unconscious of what this ennui meant, I wearied of the notion, wearied of the joyless seas of alcohol, wearied of the blunt, bluff, hearty, and totally meaningless friendships, wearied of wandering through the forests of desperate women, . . . perhaps, as we say in America, I wanted to find myself. This is an interesting phrase, not current as far as I know in the language of any other people, which certainly does not mean what it says but betrays a nagging suspicion that something has been misplaced.

(*Giovanni's Room*, pp. 30–31)

As David describes the nature of his "ennui," we hear echoes of Newman's characterization of his own boredom. He (Newman) was "sick of business," just as David is "wearied of the joyless seas of alcohol." Each character begins to apprehend the inchoate development of other aspects of his personality. Newman feels "a new man" inside his "old skin," and David says, "I wanted to find myself." What each American discovers in Paris, in his unique way, is the nature of his profound misapprehension of what it means to be an American abroad, and thus at home. David discovers also that what it means to be a man is not always clear; he explores a new foreign country, the territory of homosexual love.

The quest to find himself eventually leads David to Giovanni. They meet in a Paris bar frequented by homosexuals, where Giovanni is the bartender. Giovanni concludes at the outset that David is an American, and David tells him that he is from New York. When David tells Giovanni that New York is beautiful in a way different from Paris, Giovanni wonders how. David explains: "'It's very high and new and electric—exciting. . . . It's very twentieth century.'" In contrast, David considers Paris very old and states that one feels there "'all the time gone by,'" whereas in New York one feels "'all the time to come.'" When David tells Giovanni that he wonders what New York will become in the future, "'when the world—for Americans—is not so new,'" Giovanni does not understand. He asks David, "'You are not, are you, on another planet?'"

Through Giovanni, Baldwin strains to clarify a peculiar American phenomenon:

"The Americans are funny. You have a funny sense of time—or perhaps you have no sense of time at all, I can't tell. Time always sounds like a parade *chez vous*—a *triumphant* parade, like armies with banners entering a town. As though with enough time, and that would not need to be so very much for Americans, *n'est-ce pas?* . . . as though with enough time and all that fearful energy and virtue you people have, everything will be settled, solved, put in its place. And when I say everything . . . I mean all the serious, dreadful things, like pain and death and love, in which you Americans do not believe."

(*Giovanni's Room*, p. 51)

This scene in a gay bar—intended to represent a Jamesian international encounter—echoes Baldwin's assessment of James's achievement relative to other American novelists. Giovanni casually alludes to what Baldwin considers America's fatal flaw, its unwillingness to deal honestly with its own history. Consequently Giovanni refers to America's "funny sense of time." Americans love the electric present—the "triumphant parade." Giovanni tells David that Americans look upon the world, to recall Baldwin's criticism of Hemingway, Fitzgerald, Dos Passos, and Faulkner, "as a place to be corrected." He feels Americans believe "everything will be settled, solved, put in its place!" This can also be read, despite the philosophic nature of the conversation, as a flirtation scene.

In chapter 8 of *The American* James portrays the kind of international encounter Baldwin intends to capture when David meets Giovanni. Christopher Newman tells Count Valentin Bellegarde, the affable brother of Madame de Cintré, that he wishes to marry his sister. This surprises Count Valentin; such a proposition had not crossed his mind. He tells Newman he is not sure whether he is pleased or "horrified." He is somewhat horrified because Newman is not "noble" and does not possess "a title." Newman insists that he is as good as the next man and suggests that the count will have to prove he lacks nobility. Valentin responds, " 'That's easily done. You have manufactured washtubs.' " As the conversation proceeds, Newman delivers an extended reply that reveals his ignorance of French custom and demonstrates his sincere American attitude. After all, he does not see anything wrong with his desire to marry Madame de Cintré. This is in accord with his ambition to get "the biggest kind of entertainment a man can get. People, places, art, nature, everything."

". . . you have practically told me that your family and your friends will turn up their noses at me. I have never thought about the reasons that make it proper for people to turn up their noses, and so I can only decide the question off-hand. Looking at it in that way I can't see anything in it. I simply think, if you want to know, that I'm as good as the best. . . . To tell the truth, I have always had a rather good opinion of myself; a man who is successful can't help it."

(*The American*, p. 160)

Count Valentin listens, and, being something of a maverick, he is fascinated with what the unprecedented social situation of Newman's proposal of marriage will bring about. However, at the end of their conversation he warns Newman that he is bucking a mighty and "strange" family: " 'We are a very strange people, . . . old trees have crooked branches, old houses have queer cracks, old races have odd secrets. Remember that we are eight hundred years old!' " Thus, it is essentially because of the power and traditions and odd secrets of aristocratic French society that Newman's love goes unrequited, and his hope and expectation of marriage to Madame de Cintré remains thwarted. He is, finally, not "noble" enough, and too American. Ironically, the relationship between Newman and Count Valentin seems in some ways more intimate and more affectionate than that between Newman and Madame de Cintré. Newman and Count Valentin are able to speak man to man, in naked truth and honesty, despite their cultural and class differences. It is not altogether unlike the relationship of David to Giovanni.

As *Giovanni's Room* ends, David, "*l'americain,*" stands, as he does in the beginning, alone and naked in a big house in the south of France. Although the dramatic events that took place in Paris will doubtlessly have some effect on him, there is no clear indication that he can face his life, his past, with more honesty than before. He is, in one way or another, doomed to repeat himself. The chief artistic aim of the novel, from Baldwin's point of view, is the dramatization of an American consciousness in particular, and perhaps unusual, circumstances. The manner in which David confronts or fails to confront the reality of his life illustrates a profound aspect of collective American consciousness, an American view of the world—its righteous rhetoric notwithstanding—that holds that life is always characterized by infinite possibility, that problems, however complex, can be solved. This view of life involves a willful American blindness toward the past, whether it is the past of an individual American or the nation at large, a perspective that involves a refusal to accept the fact that a man's life, like that of a nation, is to an extraordinary degree marked by a series of past decisions. Baldwin maintains that a man's life or a nation's life is a composite of critical decisions made or not made, roads taken or not taken, and that these decisions, whether acknowledged or not, become a part of the essence of that life. Giovanni knows in his bones and blood something about the irrevocable nature of experience. He knows that after Paris, after Les Halles, after David, he can never really go home again. David, even as he searches his naked soul on the eve before the morning of Giovanni's execution, does not understand that the past never dies and never goes away. *The American*, unlike *Giovanni's Room*, is rescued from so bleak an end by Christopher Newman's special magnanimity. He, of course, fails in his attempt to break the ancient social barriers of the Bellegardes and marry Claire de Cintré, but he learns what amounts to a practical lesson about French society even if that lesson does not radically transform him.

Although Baldwin in *Giovanni's Room*, like James in *The American*, follows his protagonist from New York to Paris, another important figure is hidden beneath the carpet in *Giovanni's Room*. The fact that *Giovanni's Room* profoundly echoes *Native Son* seems to have escaped all critics of Baldwin's second novel. While apparently following the pattern of *The American*, Baldwin unconsciously displays an ambivalence toward James and a reluctant attraction to Wright and to the tradition of the protest novel. Bigger Thomas reemerges—though displaced, foreign, and racially masked—as Giovanni. *Giovanni's Room* reasserts, although via thematic variation and conflation, some of the central themes of *Native Son*. That this is not a sensational or a contrived claim becomes clear in the novel's penultimate and closing chapters, when David returns to Giovanni's room one evening after having deserted him without notice. As they engage in an intense and bitter lovers' quarrel, Giovanni reveals the story of his life before and after David. We discover that he had been a happily married man who worked in the vineyards and lived in an Italian village. His previous encounters with white Americans had been limited to tourists who visited his village; he detested them, and he tells David that he represents that type. The tourists looked upon him and his neighbors as Jan Erlone and Mary Dalton viewed Bigger and his friends when they insisted that he drive to the South Side of Chicago and take them to Ernie's Chicken Shack. Giovanni tells David:

"I can see you, many years from now, coming through our village in the ugly, fat, American motor car you will surely have by then and looking at me and looking at all of us with those empty smiles Americans wear everywhere and which you wear all the time and driving off with a great roar of the motors and a great sound of tires and telling all the other Americans you meet that they must come and see our village because it is so picturesque."

(*Giovanni's Room*, p. 203)

Giovanni bitterly resents the abstract manner in which the white American tourists misperceive his village and his life. Their "empty smiles" offend him. David "wears" the American smile and because he, like the tourists, is blinded by his national prejudice, Giovanni says, "sometimes when you smiled at me I hated you. I wanted to strike you. I wanted to make you bleed."

As quickly as Baldwin identifies Giovanni's rage and hatred with Bigger's, he attempts to rescue his character, but the addition of a different set of biographical details does not disguise the similarities. Giovanni fled his native village after his first son was "born dead," a tragedy that changed his life. Giovanni's description of his reaction to his son's death reminds us of a scene from *Native Son*: "'When I knew that it was dead, I took our crucifix off the wall and spat on it and I threw it on the floor and my mother and my girl screamed and I went out.'" Bigger Thomas also threw a cross on the floor and, as we have seen, defiantly asserted, "I can die without a cross." The symbolic significance of the two blasphemous acts is essentially the same. Hurling the symbol of Christ's body on the floor represents a dramatic suspension and defiance of familiar beliefs, a rejection of the world of their mothers and fathers. Thus, we are forced to think of Giovanni's life in a comprehensive light. This particular insistence of the narrative comes back again to *Native Son*. At the end of Baldwin's novel, Giovanni's "fate" has become the paramount issue, and, like Bigger's, his fate, excluding the possibility of divine intervention, is tragically sealed.

Giovanni's fate is revealed in the closing chapter, which essentially recapitulates the action that takes place in *Native Son* after Bigger murders Mary Dalton. After Giovanni murders his employer, Guillaume, David informs us: "It was a terrific scandal, if you were in Paris at the time you certainly heard of it, and saw the picture printed in all the newspapers of Giovanni, just after he was captured. Editorials were written and speeches were made." Like Bigger, Giovanni flees after his murder and policemen descend on the quarter as they did on the South Side of Chicago. Guillaume, it turns out, belongs like Mary Dalton to a distinguished family, and, therefore, "the dreadful whiplash of public morality" asserts itself. Just as Bigger's murder of Mary Dalton becomes a national cause célèbre, so Giovanni ignites Paris's collective opprobrium. David considers Guillaume "a disgusting old fairy," but, despite Guillaume's notorious reputation among those who share what the French sardonically call "*les goûts particuliers*," David is as astonished by the overwhelming response to his death as by the unqualified scorn exhibited toward Giovanni:

As though by some magnificently tacit agreement, with every day that he was at large, the press became more vituperative against him and more gentle towards Guillaume. It was remembered that there perished with Guillaume one of the oldest names in France. Sunday supplements were run on the history of his family. . . . It is perhaps not as incredible as it certainly seemed to me, but Guillaume's name became fantastically entangled with French history, French honor, and French glory, and very nearly became a symbol, indeed, of French manhood.

(Giovanni's Room, p. 220)

Like James in *The American,* Baldwin focuses on the status of the aristocracy in France. But even this Jamesian connection dovetails with the central theme of *Native Son*. Giovanni, like Bigger, essentially commits his crime against the state. The French, aided and abetted by the press, betray their own version of national and racial prejudice. After he is discovered in a barge tied up by the river, Giovanni is reduced in the public mind to the lowest criminal type. He loses his notorious status as a clever or cold-blooded murderer. He does not have "dash," having "gotten no further than the Seine," and thus has proved himself not a daring adventurer but "a criminal . . . of the dullest kind, a bungler."

The nature of Giovanni's desperate flight, his fugitive status, his discovery and capture, and the resulting public assessment of his character are strikingly reminiscent of Bigger's situation. Even the rodent imagery of *Native Son,* the menacing black thing that must be trapped, comes through. Baldwin provides a foreshadowing of Giovanni's fate when he and David, having just met earlier that evening, observe Paris from a taxi window. Giovanni calls Paris an "old whore" but with affection. David looks and describes what he sees:

Mist clung to the river, softening that army of trees, softening those stones, hiding the city's dreadful corkscrew alleys and dead-end streets, clinging like a curse to the men who slept beneath the bridges—one of whom flashed by beneath us, very black and lone, walking along the river.

"Some rats have gone in," said Giovanni, "and now other rats come out."

(Giovanni's Room, p. 66)

The "very black and lone" figure David and Giovanni see is a reflection of Baldwin's unconscious recollection of Bigger's lonely and desperate plight. The "rat" Giovanni sees is the ghost of Bigger Thomas. This prophetically suggests his own tragic end. Like Bigger, he is viewed as subhuman and becomes a victim of French prejudice. The French insist, for example, on robbery as the motive of Guillaume's murder. David tells Hella, his girlfriend, who has just returned from her stay in Spain, that the newspapers are not telling the truth. David becomes preoccupied, as Hella describes it, with "another truth they're not telling." This emphasis on "another truth" characterizes Baldwin's revisionary intention. In *Native Son* Wright allows the newspapers' prejudicial characterization of Bigger Thomas as a subhuman, apelike rapist to stand alone. That kind of truth, even as Wright exploits it with bold creativity, is similar, according to Baldwin, to the kind of truth Stowe proffers in *Uncle Tom's Cabin*. Stowe, dubbed "an impassioned pamphleteer" by Baldwin, tells *how* but does not reveal *why*. Similarly, Wright graphically depicts how Bigger murders Mary Dalton but merely broaches why. But, speaking of Giovanni, David reports:

The newsprint told the unforgiving world . . . in delicious detail, *how* he had done it: but not why. Why was too black for the newsprint to carry and too deep for Giovanni to tell.

I may have been the only man in Paris who knew that he had not meant to do it, who could read *why* he had done it beneath the details printed in the newsprint.

(*Giovanni's Room*, p. 224)

If we can, at least for this critical instance, allow Giovanni to stand fully as Bigger Thomas, David's preoccupation with the unexpressed significance of why Giovanni murders takes us directly back to Baldwin's principal criticism of *Native Son* in "Everybody's Protest Novel" and "Many Thousands Gone." Wright's narrator tells us that Bigger's hatred for whites (particularly Jan Erlone and Mary Dalton) was "dumb, cold, and inarticulate." In a similar way, the "truth" of Giovanni's life is "too black" and "too deep" either to be accurately portrayed by the newspapers or fully expressed by himself. Consequently, the novelist must find a strategy to render the elusive story of why Giovanni murders. Baldwin explains in "Everybody's Protest Novel," "It is this power of revelation which is the business of the novelist, this journey toward a more vast reality which must take precedence over all other claims."

Baldwin takes us beyond the headlines and newsprint by allowing David, who knows more details about the relationship between Guillaume and Giovanni than anyone, to report imaginatively what happened. Why Giovanni murders can be fully appreciated only if one has already seen the handwriting on the wall. David's account represents his own guilty memory of the dangerous side of Giovanni's personality. He knows something that very few others know about Giovanni's anger and lust, his honor and integrity. Therefore, *his* imaginative reconstruction of the murder scene has a psychological authenticity of its own. In *Giovanni's Room* no one makes lengthy arguments for or against French society or against Giovanni himself. The case is already made, indeed embedded in the text of the novel. But apart from this significant difference between the endings of *Native Son* and *Giovanni's Room*, between the portrayals of Bigger's and Giovanni's tragic fates, Baldwin distinguishes himself among his influential literary forebears. He depicts the manners and morals shared by the men with *les goûts particuliers*.

Baldwin emphasizes David's developing sexual self-consciousness—step by psychological step. The novel is essentially David's poignant and painful recollection, the night before Giovanni is scheduled to face "the knife," of what has brought him to his lonely, desperate emotional state. His telling of his story becomes an autobiographical act of contrition, an extended confession, in which he "repents." He tells us about his initial adolescent homosexual experience with a boy named Joey and the deep-seated guilt he harbored after the fact. He says, "it remained . . . at the bottom of my mind, as still and as awful as a decomposing corpse." Moreover, the novel provides poignant commentary on Western society in general—its prejudicial assumptions about homosexuals—and it displays the larger society's contradictions:

> When Guillaume's corpse was discovered it was not only the boys of the street who were frightened; they, in fact, were a good deal less frightened than the men who roamed the streets to buy them, whose careers, positions, aspirations, could never have survived such notoriety. Fathers of families, sons of great houses, and itching adventurers from Belleville were all desperately anxious that the case be closed, so that things might, in effect, go back to normal and the dreadful whiplash of public morality not fall on their backs.
>
> (*Giovanni's Room*, p. 219)

The "whiplash of public morality" figures in David's account of why Giovanni murders Guillaume.[18] In order to appreciate David's revelation of why Giovanni murders Guillaume, we need to know the history of Giovanni's and Guillaume's relationship. First, Guillaume employs Giovanni, and this reminds us of Bigger's involvement with the Daltons. Each lives at the mercy of his employer's whims. Mary Dalton forces Bigger to drive her and Jan Erlone to Ernie's Chicken Shack on the South Side of Chicago. And, later that evening, she wantonly violates social custom by sitting drunkenly in the front seat with Bigger and leaning suggestively against him. Similarly, Giovanni works as Guillaume's bartender and has to grin and bear his promiscuous, insecure, and volatile personality. Guillaume's bar tells us something about the distance of his fall from the glory of French aristocracy. David describes the bar as "a noisy, crowded, ill-lit sort of tunnel, of dubious—

or perhaps not dubious at all, or rather too emphatic—reputation." *Les folles,* the homosexual habitués, as well as a multifarious variety of types, Parisian ladies and their gigolos,
"bespectacled gentlemen," "tight-trousered boys," and a few
sailors and soldiers frequent the bar. One night David sees
Guillaume's new bartender, Giovanni. "He stood, insolent and
dark and leonine, his elbow leaning on the cash register, his
fingers playing with his chin, looking out at the crowd. It was
as though his station were a promontory and we were the
sea." But the bar, the promontory upon which Giovanni
preens, is precarious at best. In fact, it is an illusory construction inspired by the lust of the desperate hopefuls, including
Guillaume, and by Guillaume's flamboyantly theatrical style of
self-presentation. Giovanni stands, with the abandon and self-
congratulatory confidence of a blooded stallion, as Guillaume's
most attractive and coveted item. When Jacques, a friend of
Guillaume, looks delightedly at Giovanni as though he were
"a valuable race horse or a rare bit of china," Guillaume pulls
him aside and cautions him, " '*Ah, çà, mon cher, c'est strictement
du business, comprends tu?*' " Guillaume hires Giovanni because
of his striking good looks. Both parties realize this. Giovanni,
however, unlike Guillaume, does not understand the contradictory implications of the deal. He does not see or, at least,
admit to himself that if Guillaume's lust could lead to his
instant hiring, it could also, as it eventually does, lead to his
precipitous firing. Thus, Giovanni's promontory represents his
descent from traditional expectations of masculinity, a mirror
of Guillaume's fall from the grace of French aristocracy. Each
is aware, in his different way, of the exorbitant price the other
has paid to arrive at and remain in the bar. Each man tries to
remain, in desperate though different fashions, what he was
before. The murder occurs in this complicated web of social,
economic, and psychosexual circumstances.

After Guillaume becomes aware of Giovanni's and David's

relationship, he unexpectedly fires his bartender, accusing him publicly of stealing cash from the register. Giovanni's unemployment and David's subsequent abandonment lead to his rapid decline. Desperate, Giovanni turns to Jacques, and eventually becomes one of the abject street boys in the quarter.[19] Shortly thereafter, Guillaume is found dead in his private quarters above the bar. David believes that Giovanni has returned to Guillaume to get his job back and that, plying him with drinks, Guillaume has preyed upon Giovanni's sense of desperation and seduced him. Giovanni, David believes, immediately and bitterly regrets this since he has already fallen so far from his ideal of manhood; and then, "with his pleasure taken," Guillaume refuses to offer Giovanni the job. Considering that the tables of masculine pride have turned irrevocably, Guillaume gleefully and spitefully watches as Giovanni's face "grows scarlet, his voice thick." Each knows that Giovanni "like a falling movie star, has lost his drawing power." As David imagines the scene, Guillaume continues to provoke and insult Giovanni.

Giovanni certainly did not mean to do it. But he grabbed him, he struck him. And with that touch, and with each blow, the intolerable weight at the bottom of his heart began to lift: . . . Giovanni lunged after him and caught him by the sash of the dressing gown and wrapped the sash around his neck. Then he simply held on, sobbing, becoming lighter every moment as Guillaume grew heavier, tightening the sash and cursing. Then Guillaume fell. And Giovanni fell—back into the room, the streets, the world, into the presence and shadow of death.

(*Giovanni's Room,* pp. 229–30)

David's account closely parallels Wright's explanation of why Bigger murders Mary Dalton. We are told by Wright's narrator that Bigger exists at the mercy of his suppressed anger and overwhelming fear in the presence of whites. And if we accept Bigger as a symbolic personification of collective black American rage, his response to his accidental suffocation of Mary

Dalton—his lack of remorse, indeed elation and personal pride—makes sense. Wright's narrator succeeds in depicting *why* Bigger feels toward Jan Erlone and Mary Dalton that "dumb, cold, inarticulate hate." But little if anything prepares the reader for Bigger's psychological response to the murder. Fear might drive him to the extreme act of decapitating and burning Mary's body in the furnace. And an overpowering combination of rage, desperation, psychopathy, and self-hatred might drive him to rape and murder Bessie Mears. But the technical objection Baldwin raises, apart from his criticism of Max's defense of Bigger, involves Wright's failure to provide a cogent or revelatory psychological profile of Bigger. Thus, we are left to draw conclusions from his violent acts and the narrator's expository assertions.

Why does Baldwin return unconsciously to the scene? Why does he feel compelled to rewrite, indeed to repossess it? Baldwin sees that whatever technical objections he raises, the scene inspires our awe on the level of human interest or curiosity. It strikes the "what if " inclination of human consciousness. What, in fact, would happen if a young black man living during the thirties found himself in the bedroom of a drunken heiress, the daughter of his wealthy employer? And what would happen if he were detected? Would any explanation have appeared reasonable or understandable? We are swept up into the immediate suspense of the scene, the intensity of the narrative moment. Will blind Mrs. Dalton detect Bigger's presence? Will Mary struggle free and talk? And then, as Bigger perceives the weight of his deed, we realize with a shock that he has inadvertently suffocated her.

On a philosophical level, Baldwin seems attracted to the notion of visionary experiences, of resonant, life-changing moments, whether such moments arise in the context of individual lives or national life. In his essays, Baldwin affirms the possibility of individual and collective changes of minds and hearts, the possibility of human redemption through self-understanding and compassion for others. But Bigger Thomas appears beyond redemption. According to Baldwin, Bigger's "tragedy" involves his acceptance of "a theology that denies him life, that he admits the possibility of being subhuman" ("Everybody's Protest Novel," p. 23). Consequently, Baldwin tries to correct what he considers the technical failure of *Native Son* by carefully preparing us for Giovanni's tragic moment. We know that Giovanni has murdered Guillaume before David delivers his imaginary account. Nevertheless, Giovanni becomes flesh of Bigger's flesh in David's description of the murder scene. In the heat of his explosive rage, Giovanni experiences a moment of power reminiscent of Bigger's. David imagines, "with each blow, the intolerable weight at the bottom of his heart began to lift." He feels himself "becoming lighter." The daring energy Giovanni expends psychologically and figuratively propels him above and beyond the reality of the incident. But when Guillaume falls, Giovanni *also* crashes. David concludes, "And Giovanni fell back into the room, the streets, the world, into the presence and shadow of death." David's focus on "the room" and "the presence and shadow of death" constitutes a subtle transformation of Wright's handling of the moment in *Native Son*. As Wright describes Bigger's situation: "The reality of the room fell from him; the vast city of white people that sprawled outside took its place." The distinctive difference reveals two points of view. Giovanni faces "the room" and "the presence and shadow of death"; Bigger thinks of the world "outside," "the vast city of white people."

Baldwin unconsciously smuggles into *Giovanni's Room,* a place where we least expect them, *Native Son*'s central themes, images, and symbols. The comparative list is impressive: the one-room apartments, the rat imagery, the employer-employee relationships, the murders, the flight and fugitive status of the murderers, the sensational news stories, the crosses, the idolization of the murdered victim, the collective prejudice and scorn expressed for the murderer and for the group of which he is presumed to be representative. Even the airplane that soars magisterially above unemployed Bigger's head as the glamorous technological symbol of his exclusion from America's democratic promises appears indirectly in *Giovanni's Room*. When Giovanni, according to David, returns desperately to Guillaume to get his old job back, and Guillaume jokes about David's wealthy American connections, Giovanni responds, "My American ... has flown!" Guillaume replies, "The Americans always fly."

None of this, however, is intended to suggest that *Giovanni's Room* is a protest novel in the tradition of *Native Son* and *Uncle Tom's Cabin*. Baldwin's ambivalent response to James, Wright, and Stowe lends to his own work an ironic and complicated conflation of attitudes and themes that sets him apart. Take, for example, the rhetoric of redemption in *Giovanni's Room*. In a superficial way, we hear echoes of Stowe there, but when David says, in the novel's closing paragraphs, "I must believe that the heavy grace of God, which has brought me to this place, is all that can carry me out of it," his appeal is desperate, personal, and real. It does not represent Baldwin's prescription for the good or the moral life. On the contrary, Baldwin's concern—in this instance—comes closer to the moral tone of personal accountability and the ironic perception of self in relation to others that Henry James explores so dramatically and eloquently in his own work, a success that explains Baldwin's admiration for James's characterization of Strether in *The Ambassadors*.[20]

Nevertheless, Baldwin's particular angle of vision on American life makes *Giovanni's Room* his original creation, not a simple rehearsal of the themes of his powerful literary ancestors. He chooses to look through the window of American sexual customs, contradictions, and taboos. *Giovanni's Room* remains a significant text among his books because race does not appear to be a significant theme in the work. But, at bottom, it is. Baldwin subliminally conflates race and homosexuality. The novel suggests what will emerge as the preoccupation of Baldwin's later novels—*Another Country, Tell Me How Long the Train's Been Gone,* and his final novel, *Just Above My Head,* published in 1979: an explicit exploration of the homosexual as the Other, to be either granted or perpetually refused the golden promise of America's democratic dreams. To Baldwin, sex and race, in America, are hopelessly intertwined.

It should be noted that whatever may be said about traditional patterns of male bonding in American literature, Baldwin takes the theme to another exploratory level. Hawthorne's Dimmesdale and Chillingsworth, Melville's Queequeg and Ishmael, Billy Budd and Claggart, or Mark Twain's Huck and Jim may not even be precursory when viewed in relation to *Giovanni's Room.* Baldwin's depiction of Giovanni's and David's relationship prophetically anticipates the "coming out" of homosexual American men during the decades that followed. Not that the book is a thinly disguised and protracted essay on "gay rights"—packaged in fiction and set in Paris—but that it suggests the promise of another country, a new American culture in which all prejudices against others, racial and sexual, will be confronted.

CONCLUSION
The Divided Soul of James Baldwin

My progress report
concerning my journey to the palace of wisdom
is discouraging.
I lack certain indispensable aptitudes.
Furthermore, it appears
that I packed the wrong things.
I thought I packed what was necessary,
or what little I had:
but there is always something one overlooks,
something one was not told,
or did not hear.
Furthermore,
Some time ago,
I seem to have made an error in judgment,
turned this way, instead of that,
and, now, I cannot radio my position.
(I am not sure that my radio is working.
No voice has answered me for a long time now.). . .

—James Baldwin, "Inventory/On Being 52"

Twenty-odd years ago, in an essay, "Something Different, Something More," Albert Murray sharply observed that Baldwin had reneged on the artistic promise of "Everybody's Protest Novel" and "Many Thousands Gone."

Baldwin began by rejecting Wright's achievements as being inadequate and also dangerous. And at the time, as has been shown, the grounds for his rejection seemed solid enough. And besides, he himself, seemed to promise not only something different but something more. So far he has not fulfilled that promise. The only thing really to date has been his special interest in themes related to the so-called sexual revolution. . . . Otherwise, Richard Wright is the author that James Baldwin, the novelist, playwright, and spokesman, resembles more than any other, including Harriet Beecher Stowe.[1]

Murray's comments brilliantly anticipate Baldwin's complex, and perhaps inexorable, literary fate. In 1926 Langston Hughes had poignantly recognized in a famous essay, "The Negro Artist and the Racial Mountain," that "the road for the serious black artist . . . who would produce a racial art is most certainly rocky and the mountain is high."[2] But Hughes understood that an "inexhaustible supply of themes" was available to the serious black writer or artist who would genuinely attempt to catch "the innumerable overtones and undertones" of interracial relations; the writer who would capture the Afro-American's "heritage of rhythm and warmth, and his incongruous humor that so often, as in the blues, becomes ironic laughter mixed with tears."

Murray maintains that Baldwin, during the mid-sixties and

after the publication of his best sellers, *Another Country* and *The Fire Next Time,* increasingly relies on the "abstract categories of academic research . . . and less on the poetic insights of the creative artist." In a catalogue reminiscent of Hughes's "inexhaustible supply of themes," Murray essentially itemizes the absent things that never appear in Baldwin's fierce and polemical presentation of Afro-American life:

Baldwin writes about Harlem, for example, with an evangelical sense of moral outrage, and his declarations on this subject are said to have stirred the conscience of the nation. But he never really accounts for the tradition which supports Harlem's hard-headed faith in democracy, its muscular Christianity, its cultural flexibility, nor does he account for its universally celebrated commitment to elegance in motion, to colorful speech idioms, to high style, not only in personal deportment but even in the handling of mechanical devices. Intentionally or not, much of what he says implicitly denies the very existence of Harlem's fantastically knowing satire, its profound awareness and rejection of so much that is essentially ridiculous in downtown doings. Sometimes he writes as if he had never heard the comedians at the Apollo Theatre.

("Something Different," p. 119)

The young and remarkably perceptive James Baldwin, who precisely notes the limitations of *Uncle Tom's Cabin* and *Native Son,* ambivalently reflects their deep influence on him even as he scathingly criticizes them. There are aesthetic or literary as well as personal reasons for his ambivalent and paradoxical literary vision. From the outset of his career, the signature of his prose style has been an effortless facility with the rhetoric of accusation and condemnation. Perhaps it was inspired at first by the religious fervor and paternal scorn of his boyhood and, later, by his own brief stint as an adolescent preacher. Having grown up with a studied as well as emotional understanding of the mythological power of the Old Testament, he argued in "Everybody's Protest Novel" that "revelation" was "the business of the novelist, the journey toward a more vast reality which must take precedence over all other claims."

Murray, however, criticizes Baldwin's *Another Country* precisely for its failure to deliver such revelation. He sees it as lacking "the rich, complex and ambivalent sensibility of the novelist" ("Something Different," p. 118). He sees Baldwin as failing to achieve what his idol, Henry James, achieved in *The Ambassadors* and *The Turn of the Screw*: "[James] did not oversimplify the virtues of his heroes, the vice of his villains, the complexity of their situation or the ambiguity of their motives" ("Something Different," p. 120).

Whether one agrees or disagrees with Murray's assessment of *Another Country,* one sees that Baldwin's early identification with Henry James could not entirely prevail against the force of race. His idolizing of James was essentially intellectual and abstract; whereas his understanding of Stowe and Wright came from intense personal experience, from the heart. Nor is this a matter of a reductive insistence upon a simplistic duality. After all, Wright was as much an expatriate as James and perhaps even more profoundly alienated than he. But the comprehensive and daunting sense of literary *vision* that characterizes Baldwin's complex literary fate is not one of detachment, in the end. Baldwin's apprenticeship ends when he truly discovers in a Jamesian sense what it means to be James Baldwin, the famous black writer. His literary gifts become subordinate, finally, to his own ambivalent and tragic muse, as well as to his status as a literary celebrity.

By the time Baldwin is beyond his apprenticeship and approaching his middle years, he has already been typecast. His foreboding anticipation of representative status as black writer, his precautionary autobiographical words, had been made flesh. He had been an accomplice to his own categorization. But some of his earlier comments reveal his understanding of his paradoxical situation. In "The Black Boy Looks at the White Boy," his essay on Norman Mailer published in *Nobody Knows My Name*, he remarks, "The world tends to trap and immobilize you in the role you play; and it is not always easy—in fact, it is always extremely hard—to maintain a kind of watchful, mocking distance between oneself as one appears to be and oneself as one actually is" (*Nobody Knows My Name*, p. 173). Like James's Lambert Strether, Baldwin appears to recognize his literary predicament, in an emotional way, when it is far too late to turn back. So, for example, he moves from the promethean figure, the man who stole the fire of "Notes of a Native Son," the powerful writer of *The Fire Next Time*, to the embittered and self-indulgent nay-sayer of *No Name in the Street* and *Evidence of Things Not Seen*. None of Baldwin's later novels or essays rivals the narrative ingenuity and rhetorical power of *Go Tell It on the Mountain* and *Notes of a Native Son*, his first novel and his first collection of essays. Comments he makes on Henry James near the very end of his life are symptomatic of the reasons why.

In an extended interview in *The Henry James Review* in the fall of 1986, Baldwin answers a series of questions put by David Adams Leeming, who had been his secretary during the early sixties. The questions deal with the extent and nature of the influence of Henry James on his writing and on his life. In his introduction to the interview, Leeming, a James expert, tells the story of how deeply Baldwin valued a photograph of James sent to him during the early sixties by a grandson of William James, Michael James, "who had been impressed by a Civil Rights speech he heard Baldwin give in Chicago."[3] Baldwin, according to Leeming, had hung the photograph "directly above his writing desk." Leeming writes:

Baldwin and I had talked many times about James . . . and Baldwin had lectured several times on *The American, The Portrait of a Lady*, and *The Ambassadors* for my classes at Robert College in Istanbul.

In everything that he said in those conversations and those lectures, it was clear that his relationship with James was of a very special sort, perhaps of the sort that existed between James and Balzac. James was his standard—the writer he thought of when he thought of the heights to which the novelist's art might aspire.

(Interview, p. 47)

In the interview, Baldwin refers to an article entitled "The Self as Journey," which he had begun to write on James:

It strikes me that what started me on that article was some critic's comment that James had stayed in Europe describing, in effect, tea parties, while ignoring the most important event of the twentieth century, which was the American rise to dominance in world power. . . .

It seemed to me when I was reading that critic years ago that James, as I watched in *Daisy Miller*, in *The Turn of the Screw*—even in *The Turn of the Screw*, by the way, which was written, after all, by an American, and *The Wings of the Dove*, and, of course, above all in *The Ambassadors*, *The Portrait of a Lady*, and *The Princess Casamassima*—it seemed to me that in each case he was describing a certain inability (like a frozen place somewhere), a certain inability to perceive the reality of others. So that Hyacinth, for example, in *The Princess*, is never a real person to the Princess. He's an opportunity for her to discharge a certain kind of rage, a certain kind of anguish, a certain kind of bitterness about why she's become the Princess Casamassima who had been Christina Light. And she makes Hyacinth, in a sense, pay for the journey she's not been able to pay for. It seems to me that the Americans—unluckily for them—always have had a receptacle for their troubles, someone or something to pay their dues for them. . . . The white American who only became a white American once he crossed the ocean . . . always had someone else to bear the burden for him: the Indian or the "nigger." And what might have happened to him, what might have transformed him and made him grow up, happened instead to other people. It happened to Uncle Tom, it happened to Uncas, it didn't happen to him. You know, it would really be quite an extraordinary spectacle, for one sitting on Mars perhaps, to realize that the most powerful nation on Earth—the viceroy of the universe—is one of the most astounding examples of retarded adolescence in human history. It's not even a tragedy. It's far beyond that. It's a failure to see, a failure to live, a failure to be. Americans do not see me when they look at me, their kinsman—literally blood of their blood, created by them. The price they pay for living is to pretend that I'm not here, and the price they pay for that is not being able to see the world in which they live. What they don't know about me is what they don't know about Nicaragua. And it is not Nicaragua or myself who is doomed.

(Interview, pp. 49–50)

This passage reveals dramatically the glory and the tragedy of Baldwin's complex success and failure. To be sure, the preceding statement is spoken rather than written. And it certainly should not be read as though made under oath. But its metaphorical suggestions are telling. First, the scene or situation is Jamesian in a literal and figurative sense. This is, after all, a rather precious literary discussion, one only these two particular Americans can possibly have—a discussion started years before not in their native land, but in another country, another culture—in Istanbul, Turkey. This interview takes place at Baldwin's then "exile" home in St. Paul de Vence in southern France. Thus, from the start, the suggestive portrait of the artist we see framed is that of the mature writer exiled like his idol and holding forth on the apparent horrifying nature of American "innocence."

To Baldwin's and Leeming's inestimable credit, we are now the fortunate heirs of the writer's own testimony on this issue. We see, for example, that he perceptively notices a particular strength of James that many were inclined to and still do ignore. I note, in passing, that Ellison shares Baldwin's awareness of certain aspects of James's life and writing that so many critics have missed. Ellison writes:

By the time I began to write, Henry James was considered a snob, an upper-class expatriate. . . . His sensibility was considered too delicate to interest anyone who was a real man concerned with the things of this world as they existed. It was forgotten, however, that James came on the scene at a time when the abolitionists were coming in and out of his father's house, that he was part of a period in which there was great intellectual ferment, religious ferment, civil rights ferment. Few critics recalled that in that war James lost one of his older brothers, who had been a member of Colonel Shaw's Massachusetts regiment of free slaves. It was also forgotten that James's second published short story, "The Story of a Year," was based on an incident which occurred in the Civil War.[4]

Baldwin notices James's moral perspicacity and his clear vision of certain American limitations as well as Ellison did. Baldwin at first focuses on what he considers James's great gift, the ability to capture the characteristic American "inability to perceive the reality of others." This is a fine instance of Baldwin's refined literary sensibility, his precise understanding of how received cultural assumptions play themselves out in individual lives, his extraordinary intelligence of the ambiguities and contradictions of human motives.

Such particular aspects of Baldwin's sensibility, and certain proven examples—such as say, his title essay in *Notes of a Native Son*—exhibit the unequivocal grace and dignity of which he was capable. These constitute the glory of Baldwin. But there is also the tragedy. The things James believed indispensable to the profoundest portrayal of the human predicament are cast to the wind. As Baldwin continues, he forgets or dismisses the qualifying safeguards of subtlety, particularity, specificity, irony, and contradictions—what he describes in "Everybody's Protest Novel" as "something resolutely indefinable, unpredictable," as "this web of ambiguity, paradox."

The world, for Baldwin, suddenly becomes a rather small and predictable and unambiguous place of black and white certainties. We are swept up in a stormy rage of claims and assertions. America, a victim of blind racist power, has become one of the most "astounding examples of retarded adolescence in human history." And Baldwin, who in "Everybody's Protest Novel" had spoken of his commitment, "his devotion to the human being, his freedom and fulfillment; freedom which cannot be legislated, fulfillment which cannot be charted," became representative of people of color. He says, "What they don't know about me is what they don't know about Nicaragua. And it is not Nicaragua or myself who is doomed."

There is, of course, genuine merit, even if shrouded in the thick smoke of his fiery black rhetoric, in certain of his insights about America's vision of itself. There are, for example, as he observes on several occasions, people in the world who exist far beyond the confines of the American imagination. But what I call the tragedy concerns Baldwin's abdication of his responsibility as a serious writer—a serious writer like Henry James—in the course of his decision, enthusiasm, and willingness to assume the role of racial spokesman and representative. An accomplished writer and cosmopolite, Baldwin knows with acute awareness how hopelessly interdependent the world has become. If America is the premier example of "retarded adolescence," as Baldwin calls it, what country, if not his own, would he suggest even figuratively has achieved adulthood or maturity—his beloved France, England, Brazil, Nigeria? Furthermore, in "Everybody's Protest Novel" Baldwin argues passionately that a human being is considerably more than "merely a member of a Society or a Group or a deplorable conundrum to be explained by science." But he willingly becomes a representative of people of color around the globe: "What they don't know about me is what they don't know about Nicaragua."

James, like Baldwin, was preoccupied with American archetypes, as well as with issues of American national character and collective consciousness. It is hardly an accident that he chose *The American* and *The Ambassadors* as titles for his novels. He knew that geography is fate. But in James's glorious rendering of, say, Christopher Newman's or Daisy Miller's or Lambert Strether's complex American fates, nothing is lost on the central intelligence of his supersensitive narrators. We see individual American characters carrying their own baggage, each following the specific logic of their own perceptions or illusions to triumph or defeat. James writes essays about the American scene, but he rarely assumes the role of full-fledged prophet or missionary, as Baldwin did.

It seems almost as though the gods conspire against Baldwin. On the one hand, they grant him the rare and priceless gift of supreme literary intelligence. On the other, they provide a set of personal circumstances, including the historical moment, that leads him to assume the arduous task of illuminating and seeking to solve the so-called American dilemma. They made him black. To paraphrase Louis Armstrong singing "What Did I Do to Be So Black and Blue," "His only sin was in his skin." Given Baldwin's Harlem boyhood of poverty and anonymity, it makes perfect sense and it is certainly to his eternal credit that he strongly identifies with black Americans, and that he, so to speak, cut his teeth on *Uncle Tom's Cabin* and *Native Son*. It is understandable that he was inclined to exhort and persuade the hard-hearted and to articulate the rage of the disesteemed. The temper of the times, the civil rights movement, gave him the historical stage on which to voice with moral clarity and authority what the consequences of America's moral evasion and racial bigotry would be.

But finally, the threatening possibility that he clairvoyantly sees in "Everybody's Protest Novel" ensnarls him too. With the publication of *The Fire Next Time,* Baldwin is typecast as an angry spokesman—"a black Tom Paine," as *Time* magazine put it. The limitation that he had diagnosed in "Everybody's Protest Novel"—a limitation imposing itself on the writer from without and simultaneously corroborating or inscribing itself from deep within—imposed itself on him. When, after the publication of *The Fire Next Time,* he achieved a fame unprecedented for a black American writer, he achieved it, in part, because he had lost or was robbed of his identity as a writer per se. The media succeeded, at least in the popular imagination, in transforming him into an angry public spokesman. When Robert Kennedy, then attorney general, asked Baldwin to bring together a group of civil rights activists to discuss the so-called "Negro problem," he took along a mix, not only Harry Belafonte, Lena Horne, Lorraine Hansberry, and Kenneth B. Clark, but also Jerome Smith, a freedom rider; his brother, David; his literary agent; and several whites in show business. The meeting turned into a bitter shouting match. Writing of the effect of this event and what it meant for Baldwin both as writer and spokesman, the journalist W. J. Weathersby reports:

Details of the meeting and its failure leaked out to the newspapers, and Baldwin became even more of a public personality. In American life, there seem to be two stages of fame; you first of all become famous for what you do and then you reach the point . . . when what you do becomes almost irrelevant, and you are simply a celebrity. Baldwin seemed now to be reaching that second stage. His writing had been thrust into the background as the media concentrated on his activism; now his activism, his blackness, were becoming secondary to his public status: He had become a star of the gossip columns. It was possible to read the reports of the meeting with Kennedy without being aware that Baldwin was a writer.[5]

During the late sixties and seventies Baldwin assumes the role of the most famous and authoritative literary spokesman for the black cause. In his essays and interviews he by turns is extremely vituperative when speaking of white Americans and sentimental when referring to blacks. He comes across, both in his essays and interviews, as either a celebrity or angry missionary—or both.

No Name in the Street, his first major essay after *The Fire Next Time,* published in 1972, illustrates how his public position affects his sense of himself, his sense, paradoxically, of having failed the very people for whose cause he is celebrated. "I had 'made it,'" he wrote, "—that is, had been seen on television, and at Sardi's, could (presumably!) sign a check anywhere in the world, could, in short, for the length of an entrance, a dinner, or a drink, intimidate headwaiters by the use of a name which had not been mine when I was born . . . meant that I had betrayed the people who had produced me."[6]

In *No Name in the Street,* Baldwin is no longer concerned with reserving a nonracial or nonpolitical space for himself. It is no wonder, therefore, that he can make such extraordinarily despairing statements as these:

It is not necessary for a black man to hate a white man, or to have any particular feelings about him at all, in order to realize that he must kill him. Yes, we have come, or are coming to this, and there is no point in flinching before the prospect of this exceedingly cool species of fratricide—which prospect white people, after all, have brought on themselves. Of course, whenever a black man discusses violence he is said to be "advocating" it. . . . I am merely trying to face certain blunt, human facts. I do not carry a gun and do not consider myself to be a violent man: but my life has more than once depended on a gun in a brother's holster. I know that when certain blatant enemies of black people are shoveled, at last, into the ground . . . I certainly do not mourn their passing. . . . People who treat other people as less than human must not be surprised when the bread they have cast on the waters comes floating back poisoned.

(*No Name in the Street,* pp. 191–92)

Baldwin adds an epilogue to his volume. He mentions the case of Angela Davis, laments the deaths of George and Jonathan Jackson, and concludes, "There will be bloody holding actions all over the world, for years to come but the Western party is over, and the white man's sun has set. Period." These sentences could easily have been written by a Black Muslim, whose theology and mythology Baldwin himself had carefully analyzed and rejected in *The Fire Next Time.*

Clearly, Baldwin has traveled some distance from his ideal of being a writer who just happens to be black. Interviewed in his home in St. Paul de Vence by *The Black Scholar,* he said in response to a question about political themes in his work:

I also realized that to try to be a writer (which involves, after all, disturbing the peace) was political, whether one liked it or not; because if one is doing anything at all, one is trying to change the consciousness of other people. You're trying to change your own consciousness. You have to trust it to the extent—enough to begin to talk; and you talk with the intention of beginning a ferment, beginning a disturbance in someone else's mind so that he sees the situation.[7]

Baldwin's early attempt to avoid becoming "merely a Negro writer" is defined by his relentless effort to clear an imaginative space for himself. He does what many American writers before him have attempted. Irving, Hawthorne, and Melville, for example, each sought to achieve an original status as a writer in relationship to the great masters of England and Europe. However, Baldwin's situation as a black writer is Kafkaesque. His blackness allows him to see American life in an original, if alienated, way. In "Everybody's Protest Novel" and "Many Thousands Gone" he identifies uncharted literary territory that is directly related to race—both in the sense of the American "race" as distinct from European and the black as distinct from American. He says in "Many Thousands Gone," "The making of an American begins at that point where he himself rejects all other ties, any other history, and himself adopts the vesture of his adopted land." Indeed, the very titles of his novels and essays suggest a will to be an original writer in his own land— *Go Tell It on the Mountain, Notes of a Native Son, Nobody Knows My Name, Another Country.* In "A Stranger in the Village," the concluding essay in *Notes of a Native Son,* he tells the story of his stay in a Swiss village as the first and only black man in a Catholic village of five hundred that has "no movie house, no bank, no library, no theatre."[8] He arrives at a shocking recognition which he prefigures in "Autobiographical Notes," his preface to *Notes of a Native Son*:

I know, in any case, that the most crucial time in my development came when I was forced to recognize that I was a kind of bastard of the West; when I followed the line of my past I did not find myself in Europe but in Africa. And this meant that in some subtle way, in a really profound way, I brought to Shakespeare, Bach, Rembrandt, to the stones of Paris, to the cathedral at Chartres, and to the Empire State building a special attitude. These were not really my creations, they did not contain my history. . . . I was an interloper; this was not my heritage. At the same time I had no other heritage which I could possibly hope to use—I had certainly been unfitted for the jungle or the tribe. I would have to appropriate these white centuries, I would have to make them mine—I would have to accept my special attitude, my special place in this scheme.

(Notes of a Native Son, pp. 6–7)

Isolated in that Swiss village, Baldwin discovers in a profound emotional and intellectual way what it means to be a black American. He concludes that "the most illiterate" among the Swiss villagers are at home in the West, a West onto which he has been so "strangely grafted," in a way he can never be. They are connected, in a way that excludes him, to "Dante, Shakespeare, Michelangelo, Aeschylus, DaVinci, Rembrandt," among others. Yet, all the same he is really much closer to the European artists than any of the Swiss villagers—his eloquent essay is testimony to that fact. And yet his exclusion, his nagging self-conscious sense of being an "interloper," affords him a genuine literary possibility—to "appropriate" the "white centuries," "make them mine." He will "accept" his "special attitude, my special place." Baldwin's blackness distinguishes him; it offers him the opportunity to view American life from dual, if contradictory, cultural perspectives. Baldwin comments at the end of "A Stranger in the Village," and in the final paragraph of *Notes of a Native Son*:

One of the things that distinguishes Americans from other people is that no other people has ever been so deeply involved in the lives of black men, and vice versa. This fact faced, with all its implications, it can be seen that the history of the American Negro problem is not merely shameful, it is also something of an achievement. For even when the worst has been said, it must also be added that the perpetual challenge posed by this problem was always, somehow, perpetually met. It is precisely this black-white experience which may prove of indispensable value to us in the world we face today. This world is white no longer, and it will never be white again.

(*Notes of a Native Son*, p. 175)

Baldwin's black perspective, his position as a "bastard," "an interloper" in the West, separates him necessarily, irrevocably at least in this century, from the mighty Henry James. Referring to James's own situation in his interview with David Leeming, Baldwin concludes, "It seems to me that there's a distance between James and myself. I understand why he died in England as a British subject and seemed to turn his back on America." Baldwin's discovery of the inexorable artistic consequences brought on by his racial difference may be seen as a kind of loss of aesthetic innocence. Having so studiously, after the fashion of James, devoted himself to the Art of writing, now he recognizes that his race is his overwhelming artistic limitation, even as it is his profound strength. He discovers that he will be forced to work within and around this paradoxical social and aesthetic milieu, but cannot escape it. He had at first imagined a sort of inviolate artistic space, a literary garden of Eden, in which he could dwell. Some of David's comments in *Giovanni's Room* effectively suggest Baldwin's sense of what has happened to his "innocent" view of that literary garden:

Perhaps everybody has a garden of Eden, I don't know; but they have scarcely seen their garden before they see the flaming sword. Then, perhaps, life only offers the choice of remembering the garden or forgetting it. Either, or: it takes strength to remember, it takes another kind of strength to forget, it takes a hero to do both. People who remember court madness through pain, the pain of the perpetually recurring death of their innocence; people who forget court another kind of madness, the madness of the denial of pain and the hatred of innocence, and the world is mostly divided between madmen who remember and madmen who forget. Heroes are rare.

(*Giovanni's Room*, p. 37)

He wants to forget the pain occasioned by his discovery of his paradoxical literary situation, and it appears as he starts out that he may be able to do so. However, he is forced to make the most of his "special attitude," his "special place." This recurrent sense of loss of infinite artistic possibility, this poignant memory of prelapsarian desire, symbolizes as well the American dream of democratic perfection. It is a dream that Baldwin passionately affirms in the closing paragraphs of *The Fire Next Time*: "If we—and now I mean the relatively conscious whites and the relatively conscious blacks, who must, like lovers, insist on, or create, the consciousness of the others—do not falter in our duty now, we may be able . . . to end the racial nightmare, and achieve our country, and change the history of the world." Baldwin's charge as an American writer is to describe that garden, indeed help locate it again. But as a black American writer, he discovers that the garden has been hopelessly corrupted by racial arrogance and white supremacy. As he observed, perhaps like Joyce's Stephen Daedalus, he could not escape the nightmare of history because he was trapped in history and history was trapped in him. Baldwin as a writer and as a man observed America from an unusual position of denial and high fulfillment; he was thus privileged to offer special testimony on the American vision as it works itself out in tragedy and triumph. Baldwin's specific undertaking was his relentless attempt to redeem America even while he devoted himself, as best he could, to a transracial and an androgynous vision of human possibility. In that way, he fulfilled the arduous task of the American writer as Henry James described it: "We work in the dark. We do what we can. Our doubt is our passion and our passion is our task. The rest is the madness of Art."

EPILOGUE
Notes on an American Scene

When Baldwin's death on December 1, 1987, was reported on the news, friends and colleagues telephoned me. I did not know what they expected me to say. Something did happen. I began to feel an uncanny sense of intellectual disorientation. So I read the papers and listened to the news. The next day *The New York Times* proclaimed on its front page, "James Baldwin, Eloquent Essayist in Behalf of Civil Rights, Is Dead." He was eulogized in virtually all the newspapers, including *USA Today*. Documentary highlights were televised on some evening news shows. Having failed to talk with him while he was alive, I decided I had to attend the memorial service to salute him and to witness what I imagined would be an extraordinary occasion. So the evening before the funeral I flew to New York. The funeral would be held at high noon at the Cathedral Church of St. John the Divine in Manhattan, the largest Gothic cathedral in the world.

At Broadway and 110th Street I came out of the IRT subway the next day an hour or so before the funeral was to start. The sun was out. I could see construction workers moving about on the scaffolds high above the cathedral's right wing. I noticed a distant television camera swiveling in my direction as I climbed the steps. Baldwin's funeral, so *The New York Times* told me the next day, was the first held in the cathedral since Duke Ellington's in 1974. Several rows had been roped off for the press. I stood for a while and then sat in a seat directly behind the press. The front of the cathedral had been reserved for the family, friends, and honored guests. Cathedral officials and workers arranged flowers, lit candles, and went purposefully about their business. Reporters started rushing in. They focused and clicked their cameras, taking shots of the coffin bearing Baldwin's body, draped in black at the front of the cathedral. The crowd had thickened now. People were beginning to save seats for friends and relatives. I overheard an older black woman say that she knew exactly where Baldwin had grown up. She did look as if she had walked right out of the pages of *Go Tell It on the Mountain*. There were women in business suits, women with their heads wrapped in turbans, women with braided hair, glamorous black women in full-length fur coats. There were distinguished gentlemen, and other men not so well-heeled. One young black man wore a New York Yankees baseball cap, with a profusion of braids sprouting out the back.

The ushers passed out the memorial programs. One woman with blond hair directly in front of me took four. JAMES ARTHUR BALDWIN 1924–1987 was printed in bold black across the top. Three photographs were beneath his name: an ascoted graying Baldwin, sitting with his hands crossed, looking fierce with his wrinkled brow; a close-up of Baldwin's face with eyes full of compassion; and a group photograph of Charlton Heston, Harry Belafonte, Marlon Brando, and Baldwin, all smiling at Washington's Lincoln Memorial, and with a caption referring to the "turbulent sixties." Perhaps it was at the March on Washington led by Dr. Martin Luther King. Lincoln's head behind was like a gray and immovable ghost. Baldwin is smiling broadly, Brando has his arm around him. I remembered one of Baldwin's essays in which he told how Brando loaned him five hundred dollars when he was down and out in Paris. The bottom of the program had a passage from Baldwin's short story "Sonny's Blues." "For, while the tale of how we suffer and how we are delighted, and how we may triumph is never new, it always must be heard. There isn't any other tale to tell, it's the only light we've got in all this darkness. And this tale, according to that face, that body, those strong hands on those strings, has another aspect in every country, and a new depth in every generation." There was a full-page eulogy, "Jimmy," by Amiri Baraka. The program announced that the "Encomium/Tributes" would be delivered by Toni Morrison, Maya Angelou, and His Excellency Emmanuel de Margerie, Ambassador of France.

When I looked up from the program, I saw thousands— more blacks than whites. Then precisely at noon the organ began. There was something authoritative, grand, and yet deeply forlorn about the soaring sound that charged the cathedral air with its own mysterious power. The notes, the soaring sound, seemed to possess an unimpeachable knowledge of life's horror and glory. They had been through it all; the notes seemed to say: birth, marriage, death, and death again. They had known it all already. The organ music faded away. I heard drums and saw the Very Reverend James P. Morton, Dean of the cathedral, leading the procession, followed by the cathedral choirs in white and maroon robes. The grief-stricken family and friends were coming down the aisle, moving with grace and dignity through the crowd. Maya Angelou looked hurt. Toni Morrison, with her impressive gray hair, seemed propelled by an extraterrestrial force. Amiri Baraka marched with the pugnacious attitude of a soldier; he could have been a decorated veteran in a Memorial Day parade.

After the procession came anthems and prayers. The cathedral choirs sang the Twenty-third Psalm. Odetta rose and sang a haunting medley of familiar songs, "The Battle Hymn of the Republic" and "Let Us Break Bread Together" among them. The audience joined in, and many began to weep. Her voice created an aura of intimacy among the thousands there. I wondered who among this vast crowd, beyond his immediate family, had truly known this remarkable man? And how did they feel—those who had been the object and subject of his great passions?

Maya Angelou spoke first. She assumed the role of Baldwin's little sister. She warned us at the outset of how Baldwin's name would be used in vain: "Some fantasies will be broadcast and even some truths will be told." She told how Baldwin had showered her with his fraternal gifts: "He furnished me with my first limousine ride, set the stage for me to write 'I Know Why the Caged Bird Sings.' . . . I knew that he knew black women may find lovers on street corners or even in church pews, but brothers are hard to come by and are as necessary as air and as precious as love."

Toni Morrison spoke next. Her voice was firm yet deeply sensitive. In a sense, she was writing an extended thank you note to her older dead brother: "Jimmy, there is too much to think about you, and too much to feel. The difficulty is your life refuses summation—it always did—and invites contemplation instead." She was poignantly sharp in her description of Baldwin's contribution to American English. "You stripped it of its ease and false comfort and fake innocence and evasion and hypocrisy. And in place of deviousness was clarity. In place of soft plump lies was a lean, targeted power."

Emmanuel de Margerie, the French ambassador to the United States, spoke warmly and briefly of the love and grief of France. He was followed by a "Horn Salute," Hugh Masakela on trumpet, Jimmy Owens on flügelhorn, Danny Nixon on piano, playing a mixed medley, including a spirited rendition of "When the Saints Go Marching In."

Amiri Baraka spoke next. In a fervent exhortatory tone and in the incantatory rhythms of the poets of the sixties, he too portrayed Baldwin as his "older brother." There was poetic precision and insight in the smoke of his rapid rhetoric: "When we saw and heard him, he made us feel good. He made us feel, for one thing, that we could defend ourselves or define ourselves, that we were in the world not merely as animate slaves, but as terrifyingly sensitive measurers of what is good or evil, beautiful or ugly. . . . This is the fire that terrifies our pitiful enemies. That not only are we alive but shatteringly precise in our songs and our scorn."

Then we heard Baldwin singing "Precious Lord." His baritone voice was issuing forth disembodied as though self-generating out of the cathedral air, no music—no organ, no trumpet, no drum—just the voice coming to us: "Precious Lord, take my hand; lead me on; let me stand. I am tired. I am weak. I am worn." I listened to the haunting, majestic song. And it occurred to me that Baldwin's final testimony at his final hour was his own clear black song of faith. He was leaving this behind to guide us through the threatening chaos. And faith, as he so profoundly knew, "is the substance of things hoped for, the evidence of things not seen."

The rest of the service, the singing of the choirs, the benediction, washed past me. And before I knew it I heard the drums of Babatunde Olatunji again. The retiring procession had begun. Baldwin's coffin was wheeled past us. And then I saw her, Baldwin's mother, being pushed slowly past us in a wheelchair. She wore a black pillbox hat with a striking gem. She was sobbing in a deep and dignified way. I saw those eyes—the eyes that Baldwin concluded had deeply inspired his stepfather's resentment; those eyes that had made Baldwin famous. They were so clearly Baldwin's eyes as they were hers. This stunning recognition, this confirmation, made me cry. I wondered what Emma Baldwin was thinking, whether the occasion inspired her fondest memories of Jimmy, the eldest of her nine children. Yes, I wondered what that little old black lady thought, weeping and yet clinging to her monumental dignity, as the final whirlwind of her famous son's magnificent and stormy life blew past her.

I came out of the cathedral somewhat dazed. I still heard the rhythmic cadences of the drums. The winter sun was bright and invigorating, a symbolic benediction for us all. There was a long line of black cars parked in front of the cathedral. The event had been breathtaking for me, the pre-sumptuous literary critic. John Grimes's hilltop fantasy, his glowing American dream, in Central Park had been made real. So in *Go Tell It on the Mountain,* his first book, Baldwin had prophetically spelled out, in his beginning, his magnificent end: "He would be, of all, the mightiest, the most beloved, the Lord's anointed; and he would live in this shining city which his ancestors had seen with longing from far away. For it was his; the inhabitants of the city had told him it was his; he had but to run down, crying, and they would take him to their hearts and show him wonders his eyes had never seen."

Then I overheard the mannered voice of a black man in his fifties holding forth. He spoke with brash, know-it-all cer-tainty. I gathered that he had "viewed the body" the evening before. He reported to all of us in his immediate vicinity that Baldwin had been "put away" in a "nice box." He said it had been brought back from France. The next day, Lee A. Daniels described the "nice box" in *The New York Times.* "The coffin bearing Mr. Baldwin's body was of gleaming mahogany with a brass cross and plaque on its top bearing the words 'James A. Baldwin, 1924–1987.' It was brought into the cathedral more than an hour before the service and draped with a rich black pall."

A few steps away, an attractive black woman in her twenties, her lips faultlessly painted red, smiled at me and, with a cameraman following, framed and entrapped me. "Sir," she said, pushing her microphone to my lips, "what do you think of this?" With the camera pointing, it seemed, down to my tonsils, I said I was down from New Hampshire; I had come down because Baldwin was an important writer. She turned abruptly and shouted to her cameraman in a clipped tone, "Look! Get Cicely Tyson over there! OVER THERE!" But the door of the car was closing. "It's too late now," she said in a tone of disgust at her assistant's apparent incompetence. "Come back to him," she said to the cameraman. I do not recall what else I said. But it was brief and general. Then they left me alone. The procession of black cars was beginning to leave. They were taking James Arthur Baldwin home to Harlem one last time.

In the midst of the voices, I remembered the writer singing:

> Precious Lord,
> take my hand.
> Lead me on,
> let me stand.
> I am tired.
> I am weak.
> I am worn.
>
> Through the storm,
> through the night,
> lead me on to the light.
> Precious Lord,
> take my hand—
> Lead me home.

NOTES

Preface

1. Harold Bloom, *The Anxiety of Influence: A Theory of Poetry* (New York: Oxford University Press, 1973).
2. Vincent B. Leitch, *Deconstructive Criticism: An Advanced Introduction* (New York: Columbia University Press, 1983), p. 136.

Introduction

1. Jordan Elgrably, "The Art of Fiction LXXVII: James Baldwin," *The Paris Review* 26 (Spring 1984), p. 59.
2. James Baldwin, *Go Tell It on the Mountain* (New York: Dell Publishing Co., 1953).
3. James Baldwin, *The Fire Next Time* (New York: The Dial Press, 1963).
4. "Birmingham and Beyond: The Negro's Push for Equality," *Time* 81 (May 17, 1963), p. 8.
5. James Baldwin, *Nobody Knows My Name: More Notes of a Native Son* (New York: Dell Publishing Co., 1961), p. 17.
6. W. E. B. Du Bois, "The Social Origins of American Negro Art," *Modern Quarterly* 3 (October–December, 1925), pp. 53–56.
7. Stanley Macebuh, *James Baldwin: A Critical Study* (New York: The Third Press, 1973).
8. Louis H. Pratt, *James Baldwin* (Boston: Twayne Publishers, 1978).
9. Carolyn Wedin Sylvander, *James Baldwin* (New York: Frederick Ungar Publishing Co., 1980).
10. Trudier Harris, *Black Women in the Fiction of James Baldwin* (Knoxville: The University of Tennessee Press, 1985).
11. Pratt, *Baldwin*, pp. 50–51.
12. Macebuh, *Baldwin*, p. 33.
13. Macebuh, *Baldwin*, p. 167.

14. Macebuh, *Baldwin,* p. 167.
15. Michel Fabre, "Fathers and Sons in James Baldwin's *Go Tell It on the Mountain,*" in Keneth Kinnamon, ed. *James Baldwin: A Collection of Critical Essays* (Englewood Cliffs: Prentice-Hall, Inc., 1974).

I. *"A Rage in the Blood"*

1. James Baldwin, *Notes of a Native Son* (Boston: Beacon Press, 1955, 1984).
2. Richard Wright, *Native Son* (New York: Harper & Row, 1940, 1966).

II. *"This Web of Lust and Fury"*

1. The American version of "Everybody's Protest Novel" appeared in *Partisan Review,* June 1949. But the essay first appeared in *Zero,* a small French magazine. Ironically, Wright asked the editor of *Zero* to publish Baldwin's article, although he was unaware at the time of the latter's critical comments on *Native Son.* For a fuller discussion of this issue, see Michel Fabre, *The Unfinished Quest of Richard Wright* (New York: William Morrow & Co., Inc., 1973), pp. 362–63; see Irving Howe, "James Baldwin: At Ease in Apocalypse," *James Baldwin: A Collection of Critical Essays,* ed. Keneth Kinnamon (Englewood Cliffs, N.J.: Prentice-Hall, Inc., 1974), p. 97.
2. The work of Macebuh and Pratt are representative examples.
3. James Baldwin, "Everybody's Protest Novel," *Notes of a Native Son* (Boston: Beacon Press, 1955, 1984), pp. 15–16.
4. Jane Tompkins, *Sensational Designs: The Cultural Work of American Fiction, 1790–1860* (New York: Oxford University Press, 1985).
5. Ibid., p. 122.   6. Ibid., p. 123.
7. Tompkins argues that *Uncle Tom's Cabin* "stands opposed to works like [George Eliot's] *Middlemarch* and [Henry James's] *The Portrait of a Lady* in which everything depends on human action unfolding in a temporal sequence that withholds revelation until the final moment." Tompkins, *Sensational Designs,* p. 134.
8. Ibid., p. 135.   9. Ibid., pp. 141–42.
10. Ibid., p. 141.   11. Ibid., p. xi.
12. Leslie A. Fiedler, *The Inadvertent Epic: From* Uncle Tom's Cabin *to* Roots (New York: Simon and Schuster, 1979).
13. Ibid., p. 16.   14. Ibid., p. 17.
15. Ibid., p. 27.
16. Alexis de Tocqueville, *Democracy in America* (New York: Vintage Books, 1945), pp. 343–452.
17. Robert B. Stepto, *From Behind the Veil: A Study of Afro-American Narrative* (Urbana: University of Illinois Press, 1979).

18. *Slave Testimony: Two Centuries of Letters, Speeches, Interviews, and Auto-biographies,* ed. John W. Blassingame (Baton Rouge: Louisiana State University Press, 1977), p. xli.
19. Thomas F. Gossett, *Uncle Tom's Cabin and American Culture* (Dallas: The Southern Methodist University Press, 1985), pp. 107–8.
20. Frederick Douglass, *Narrative of Life of Frederick Douglass, An American Slave, Written by Himself* (New York: Doubleday, 1845, 1963); William Craft, *Running a Thousand Miles for Freedom: Or the Escape of William and Ellen Craft from Slavery* (New York: Arno, 1860, 1970); Harriet Brent Jacobs, *Incidents in the Life of a Slave Girl: Mrs. Harriet Brent Jacobs, Written by Herself* (New York: AMS Press, 1861, 1973). Although Craft's and Brent's narratives were published after *Uncle Tom's Cabin,* we know that many of the slaves wrote their stories years after delivering lectures before various antislavery societies. Thus, their stories were a part of an abolitionist oral history. Moreover, in the specific case of Brent, she lived with a distinguished abolitionist family for over a decade before writing her narratives.
21. Thomas F. Gossett, *Uncle Tom's Cabin and American Culture* (Dallas: Southern Methodist University Press, 1985), p. 3.
22. James Baldwin, *The Fire Next Time* (New York: The Dial Press, 1963), p. 119.
23. Harriet Beecher Stowe, *Uncle Tom's Cabin* (New York: New American Library, 1966), p. v.

III. "My Ally, My Witness, and Alas! My Father"

1. Houston Baker, Jr. *Blues, Ideology, and Afro-American Literature: A Vernacular Theory* (Chicago: The University of Chicago Press, 1984).
2. According to Baker, a black hole has four salient, though invisible, features: 1) "The area marked by the black hole is dark because an initially luminescent star has, in its burning, converted energy to mass"; 2) ". . . while the black hole is darkly invisible, it is detectable by the energy field resulting from its attraction of hydrogen atoms, cosmic particles, and other objects"; 3) "The gravitation is so forceful that it not only attracts cosmic particles but also may hold another massive, luminous star in a binary system"; and 4) "They [black holes] are surrounded by an 'event horizon,' a membrane that prevents the unaltered escape of anything which passes through." Baker, *Blues, Ideology,* pp. 144–45.
3. Ibid., p. 140.
4. Houston A. Baker, Jr., *The Journey Back: Issues in Black Literature and Criticism* (Chicago: The University of Chicago Press, 1980). Baker's comments in this earlier work are considerably more in tune with my

own views on Baldwin. His comments on *Giovanni's Room*, for example, anticipate my own. See especially pp. 60–64 and 113–17.

5. James Baldwin, "Alas, Poor Richard," *Nobody Knows My Name: More Notes of a Native Son* (New York: The Dial Press, 1961), pp. 148–49.

6. Eldridge Cleaver, *Soul on Ice* (New York: Dell Publishing, 1968), pp. 97–111.

7. Baker, *Blues, Ideology,* pp. 142–43.

8. Alfred Kazin, *New York Jew* (New York: Vintage Books, 1978), pp. 65–67.

9. Baker uses the term "black blues life" throughout *Blues, Ideology* to characterize the quintessential nature of Wright's life.

10. James Baldwin, "The Discovery of What It Means to Be an American," *Nobody Knows My Name: More Notes of a Native Son* (New York: The Dial Press, 1961), p. 18.

11. James Baldwin, "Many Thousands Gone," *Notes of a Native Son* (Boston: Beacon Press, 1955, 1984).

12. For perceptive defenses of Wright's achievement in *Native Son,* see Donald Gibson's "Wright's Invisible Native Son" and Paul N. Siegel's "The Conclusion of Richard Wright's Native Son," *Richard Wright: A Collection of Critical Essays,* eds. Richard Macksey and Frank E. Moorer (New York: Prentice-Hall, 1984), pp. 95–106, 106–17. For a representative discussion of *Native Son*'s limitations, see Edward Margolies, *The Art of Richard Wright* (Carbondale: Southern Illinois University Press, 1969), pp. 114–15.

13. Thus, at first, Baldwin's ethnicity was questionable. This phenomenon of black American writers shielding their race from the reading public is not entirely new. During the late nineteenth century and the first decades of the twentieth, Charles Chesnutt, Paul Laurence Dunbar, and James Weldon Johnson faced a similar problem. But those writers were trying to avoid being completely "blacklisted" in the literary marketplace. Baldwin's situation was somewhat different.

14. Jordan Elgrably, "The Art of Fiction LXXVII," *The Paris Review* 26 (Spring 1984), p. 81.

15. James laments the arid creative climate in which his precursor Nathaniel Hawthorne wrote. He concludes that America had "No sovereign, no court, no personal loyalty, no aristocracy, no church, no clergy, no army, no diplomatic service, no country gentlemen, no palaces, no castles . . . no literature, no novels, no museums, no pictures. . . ." *Theory of Fiction: Henry James,* ed. James E. Miller, Jr. (Lincoln: University of Nebraska Press, 1972), p. 49.

16. Richard Wright, *Black Boy* (New York: Harper & Row, 1945, 1966), p. 45.

17. Richard Wright, *Native Son* (New York: Harper & Row, 1940, 1966), p. 68.

18. James Baldwin, "Previous Condition," *Going to Meet the Man* (New York: Dell Publishing Co., Inc., 1965, 1969). "Previous Condition" was first published in *Commentary*, October 1948.

IV. The "Bitter Nourishment" of Art

1. Richard Wright, *American Hunger* (New York: Harper & Row, 1977), p. 63.
2. See Robert B. Stepto's *From Behind the Veil: A Study of Afro-American Narrative* (Urbana: University of Illinois Press). Stepto writes: "Afro-American culture, like all cultures, has its store of what Northrup Frye has called 'canonical stories' or what I call 'pregeneric myths'—shared stories or myths that not only exist prior to literary form but eventually shape the forms that comprise a given culture's literary canon. The primary pregeneric myth for Afro-America is the quest for freedom and literacy."
3. One does not immediately think of Jamesian encounter scenes, say, Lambert Strether observing and shockingly recognizing the significance of Chad Newsome and Madame de Vionnet being in the same boat in the scene at the Cheval Blanc. But we appreciate this framed scene all the more because James has studiously prepared us for it.
   Baldwin also arranges his narrative so that each new revelation enhances our sense of the characters we are getting to know. John, the protagonist, son of Richard and Elizabeth, is the first character we see and observe. Our initial encounter with John comes before we know of his dead biological father, Richard.
4. W. E. B. Du Bois, *The Souls of Black Folk* (1903, Reprint Greenwich CT: Fawcett, 1961), p. 17.
5. See "Perspective of Literature" in Ralph Ellison's *Going to the Territory* (New York: Random House, 1986, p. 335). Ellison writes: "Ironically, however, this initial act of pride was to give the Afro-American an inadvertent and unrecognized but crucial role in the nation's drama of conscience. . . .
   "As a symbol of guilt and redemption, the Negro entered the deepest recesses of the American psyche and became crucially involved in its consciousness, subconsciousness, and conscience. He became keeper of the nation's sense of democratic achievement, the human scale by which would be measured its painfully slow advance toward true equality."

V. "Out of Disorder, the Order Which Is Art"

1. James Baldwin, "As Much Truth as One Can Bear," *New York Times Book Review*, January 14, 1962, p. 1.

2. Ibid., p. 1.

3. Fern Marja Eckman, *The Furious Passage of James Baldwin* (New York: M. Evans & Co., 1966), p. 169.

4. Jordan Elgrably, "The Art of Fiction LXXVII," *The Paris Review,* 26 (Spring 1984), p. 54.

5. James Miller provides a succinct, definitive difference: "for life itself, the important terms are *immediacy* and *application*: for art, these become *reflection* and *appreciation*. We are involved in the action of life, and must act and apply; we are interested in the action of fiction (if we are), and appreciate it most intensely in its reflections on the feelings and thoughts of characters." *Theory of Fiction: Henry James,* ed. James E. Miller, Jr. (Lincoln: University of Nebraska Press, 1972), p. 16.

6. Henry James, *The Art of the Novel: Critical Prefaces* (New York: Charles Scribner's, 1934), p. 46.

7. Baldwin actually wrote *The Amen Corner* in 1954 after completing *Go Tell It on the Mountain*. It was produced at Howard in 1956 and later published.

8. James Baldwin, *Notes of a Native Son* (Boston: Beacon Press, 1955, 1984), p. 7.

9. Henry James, *The American* (New York: Penguin Books, 1983). William Spengemann provides a thoughtful introduction to and annotates this edition.

10. Spengemann's introduction to *The American,* pp. 15–16.

11. James Baldwin, *Giovanni's Room* (New York: The Dial Press, 1956).

12. Robert Bone, *The Negro Novel in America,* rev. ed. (New Haven: Yale University Press, 1965).

13. Bone, *Negro Novel,* p. 226.

14. Roger Austen, *Playing the Game: The Homosexual Novel in America* (Indianapolis: Bobbs-Merrill Co., 1977), p. 150.

15. *The American* is not, to be sure, the story of a peculiarly American form of sexual confusion but of social innocence, which in Paris amounts to social confusion. Christopher Newman, an attractive and wealthy bachelor, decides to travel to Paris in order to saturate himself with high culture and find a wife, "the best article in the market." Eventually he is introduced to Claire de Cintré, an aristocratic young widow to whom he, after a complicated courtship, proposes marriage. She tells him to hold off for six months. She eventually accepts, but, pressured by her family, the powerful Bellegardes, changes her mind. Newman discovers a scandalous family secret and threatens revenge. Madame de Cintré joins a convent. The novel ends with Newman throwing the letter that could have destroyed the social standing of the Bellegardes into the fire. His is the story of an American love thwarted by innocent, though presumptuous, American social expectations.

16. Henry James, *The Future of the Novel: Essays on the Art of Fiction*, ed. Leon Edel (New York: Vintage Books, 1956), p. 126.

17. James, *Critical Prefaces*, pp. 21–22.

18. Trudier Harris, *Exorcising Blackness: Historical and Literary Lynching and Burning Rituals* (Bloomington: Indiana University Press, 1984). Harris discusses the mob's response to Bigger Thomas; see especially pp. 112–14.

19. We may note in passing, as Colin MacInnes also observes, that Baldwin's characterization of Giovanni at this point in the novel is questionable. Nothing in the novel prepares us for Giovanni's—the "insolent and leonine" ex-husband—precipitous fall, so to speak, to his knees. See Colin MacInnes, "Dark Angel: The Writings of James Baldwin," *Five Black Writers: Essays on Wright, Ellison, Baldwin, Hughes, and Leroi Jones,* ed. Donald B. Gibson (New York: New York University Press, 1970), p. 129.

20. For further discussion of this issue see Charles Newman, "The Lesson of the Master: Henry James and James Baldwin," *Yale Review* 56 (October 1966), pp. 45–59 and Lyall Powers, "Henry James and James Baldwin: The Complex Figure," *Modern Fiction Studies* 30 (Winter 1984), pp. 651–67.

Conclusion: The Divided Soul of James Baldwin

1. Albert Murray, "Something Different, Something More," in Herbert Hill, ed., *Anger, and Beyond: The Negro Writer in the United States* (New York: Harper & Row, 1966), p. 133–34.

2. Langston Hughes, "The Negro Artist and the Racial Mountain," in John A. Williams and Charles F. Harris, eds., *Amistad I* (New York: Vintage Press, 1970), p. 303.

3. David Adams Leeming, "An Interview with James Baldwin on Henry James," *The Henry James Review* 8 (1986), p. 47.

4. Ralph Ellison, "The Novel as a Function of Democracy," in *Going to the Territory* (New York: Random House, 1986), pp. 312–13.

5. W. J. Weathersby, *Squaring Off: Mailer vs. Baldwin* (New York: Mason/ Charter, 1977), p. 96.

6. James Baldwin, *No Name in the Street* (New York: The Dial Press, 1972; Delta edition, 1973), p. 12.

7. "*The Black Scholar* Interviews James Baldwin," *The Black Scholar* 5 (December–January, 1974), p. 40.

8. James Baldwin, "A Stranger in the Village," in *Notes of a Native Son.* This essay is one of Baldwin's most poignant discussions of the contradictory nature of the Afro-American presence in the Western world.

JAMES BALDWIN: A SELECTED BIBLIOGRAPHY

1. Works by James Baldwin

Novels and Short Stories

Another Country. New York: Dial Press, 1962.

"The Death of the Prophet." *Commentary* 9 (March 1950): 257–61.

Giovanni's Room. New York: Dial Press, 1956.

Going to Meet the Man. New York: Dial Press, 1965.

Go Tell It on the Mountain. New York: Alfred A. Knopf, 1953

If Beale Street Could Talk. New York: Dial Press, 1974.

Just Above My Head. New York: Dial Press, 1979.

Little Man, Little Man: A Story of Childhood. New York: Dial Press, 1976.

Tell Me How Long the Train's Been Gone. New York: Dial Press, 1968.

Essays and Dialogues

The Devil Finds Work: An Essay. New York: Dial Press, 1976.

A Dialogue: James Baldwin and Nikki Giovanni. Philadelphia: J. B. Lippincott, 1973.

Evidence of Things Not Seen. New York: St. Martin's/Marek, 1985.

The Fire Next Time. New York: Dial Press, 1963.

Nobody Knows My Name: More Notes of a Native Son. New York: Dial Press, 1961.

No Name in the Street. New York: Dial Press, 1972.

Notes of a Native Son. Boston: Beacon Press, 1955.

Baldwin, James, and Avedon, Richard. *Nothing Personal.* New York: Atheneum Publishers, 1964.

The Price of the Ticket. New York: St. Martin's/Marek, 1985.

A Rap on Race: Margaret Mead and James Baldwin. Philadelphia: J. B. Lippincott, 1971.

Plays and Scenarios

The Amen Corner. New York: Dial Press, 1968.
Blues for Mister Charlie. New York: Dial Press, 1964.
One Day, When I Was Lost: A Scenario Based on Alex Haley's "The Autobiography of Malcolm X." London: Michael Joseph, 1972.

Poetry

Jimmy's Blues. New York: St. Martin's/Marek, 1985.

Discussions and Interviews

Baldwin, James, and Buckley, William F., Jr. "The American Dream and the American Negro." *New York Times Magazine,* 7 March 1965, pp. 32–33, 87–89.
Baldwin, James, and Clark, Kenneth. "New York Negroes and Bobby—Both Shocked." Interviewed by Sue Solet. *New York Herald Tribune,* 29 May 1963, p. 1.
Baldwin, James; Glazer, Nathan; Hook, Sidney; and Myrdal, Gunnar. "Liberalism and the Negro: A Round-Table Discussion." *Commentary* 37 (March 1964): 25–42.
Baldwin, James; Hansberry, Lorraine; Hughes, Langston; Kazin, Alfred; Capouya, Emile; and Hentoff, Nat. *Cross Currents* 11 (Summer 1961): 205–24.
Baldwin, James; Mossman, James; and MacInnes, Colin. "Race, Hate, Sex, and Colour: A Conversation." *Encounter* 25 (July 1975): 55–60.
Baldwin, James; Worsthorne, Peregrine; and Magee, Bryan. "'Let me finish, let me finish . . . ,' A Television Conversation." *Encounter* 39 (September 1972): 27–33.
"Are We on the Edge of Civil War?" In *The Americans,* interviewed by David Frost, pp. 145–50. New York: Stein and Day Publishers, 1970.
"The Art of Fiction LXXVIII: James Baldwin." Interviewed by Jordan Elgrably. *The Paris Review* 26 (Spring 1984): 48–82.
"At a Crucial Time a Negro Talks Tough: 'There's a Bill Due That Has To Be Paid.'" *Life,* 24 May 1963, pp. 81–86A.
"The Author Speaks." *New York Herald Tribune Books,* 17 June 1962, p. 3.
"Black Man in America: An Interview by Studs Terkel." *WFMT Perspectives* 10 (December 1961): 28–39.
"*The Black Scholar* Interviews: James Baldwin" *Black Scholar* 5 (December–January 1974): 33–42.
"A Conversation with James Baldwin." Interviewed by Kenneth B. Clark. *Freedomways* 3 (Summer 1963): 361–68.
"Dialog in Black and White: James Baldwin and Budd Schulberg." *Playboy* 13 (December 1966): 33–36.
"Disturber of the Peace: James Baldwin." Interviewed by Eve Auchincloss

and Nancy Lynch. In *The Black American Writer*, Vol. I, edited by C. W. E. Bigsby, pp. 199–216. Deland, Florida: Everett/Edwards, 1969.

"Exclusive Interview with James Baldwin." Interviewed by Joe Walker. *Muhammad Speaks*, 8, 15, 22, 29 September 1972.

"How Can We Get the Black People to Cool It? An Interview with James Baldwin." *Esquire* 70 (July 1968): 49–53.

"The Image: Three Views, from Messrs. Shahn, Milhoud, Baldwin; Three Creative Artists Debate the Meanings of a Fashionable Term." *Opera News* 27 (8 December 1962): 8–13.

"An Interview with a Negro Intellectual." In *The Negro Protest: Talks with James Baldwin, Malcolm X, Martin Luther King*, edited by Kenneth B. Clark, pp. 1–14, 49. Boston: Beacon Press, 1963.

"An Interview with James Baldwin." Interviewed by David C. Estes. *New Orleans Review* 13 (Fall 1986): 59–64.

"An Interview with James Baldwin on Henry James." Interviewed by David Adams Leeming. *The Henry James Review* 8 (Fall 1986): 47–56.

"An Interview with Josephine Baker and James Baldwin." Interviewed by Henry Louis Gates, Jr; Anthony Barthelemy, ed. *The Southern Review* 21 (Summer 1985): 594–602.

"It's Hard To Be James Baldwin: An Interview." Interviewed by Herbert R. Lottman. *Intellectual Digest* 2 (July 1972): 67–68.

"James Baldwin Breaks His Silence." *Atlas* 13 (March 1967): 47–49.

"James Baldwin Comes Home." Interviewed by Jewell Hardy Gresham. *Essence*, 7 June 1976, p. 54.

"James Baldwin—Henri Alleg: People Must Not Lose Each Other." *World Marxist Review* 30 (November 1987): 149–54.

"James Baldwin . . . in Conversation." Interviewed by Dan Georgakas. In *Black Voices: An Anthology of Afro-American Literature*, edited by Abraham Chapman, pp. 660–668. New York: New American Library, 1968.

"James Baldwin, the Renowned Black American Novelist, Talks to Godwin Matatu." *Africa: International Business, Economic and Political Monthly* 37 (1974): 68–69.

"James Baldwin: Une Interview Exclusive." Interviewed by Nobile Fares. *Jeune Afrique* 1 (September 1970): 20–24.

"James Baldwin: Une Interview par Guy Le Clec'h." *Le Figaro Literaire* 19 (23–30 September 1964): 4–5.

"'The News from All the Northern Cities Is, to Understate It, Grim; the State of the Union is Catastrophic.'" *New York Times*, 5 April 1978, p. A29.

"Of Angela Davis and 'the Jewish Housewife Headed for Dachau': An Exchange—James Baldwin and Shloma Katz." *Midstream* 17 (June–July 1971): 3–7.

"Pour Liberer les Blancs." Interviewed by François Bondy. *Prevues* 152 (1963): 3–17.

"T.V. and Radio: An Interview with James Baldwin." Interviewed by Robert Lewis Shayon. *Saturday Review* 45 (24 February 1962): 35.

"Une Recontre Avec James Baldwin." *L'Afrique Litteraire et Artistique* 38 (1975): 51–54.

"'We Are all the Viet Cong!': An Interview with James Baldwin." Interviewed by Karen Wald. *Nickel Review* 4 (27 February 1970): 5.

"What's the Reason Why? A Symposium by Best Selling Authors." *New York Times Book Review*, 2 December 1962, p. 3.

"When a Pariah Becomes a Celebrity: An Interview with James Baldwin." Interviewed by Clayton G. Holloway. *Xavier Review* 7 (1987): 1–10.

'Why I Left America: Conversation: Ida Lewis and James Baldwin." In *New Black Voices*, edited by Abraham Chapman, pp. 409–19.

"Writer Foresees Collision Course." Interviewed by Nick Ludington. *The Washington Post*, 14 December 1969, p. E8.

Other Works

"Among the Recent Letters to the Editor." *New York Times Book Review*, 26 February 1961, pp. 52–53.

"Anti-Semitism and Black Power." *Freedomways* 7 (Winter 1967): 75–77.

"The Artist's Struggle for Integrity." *Liberation* 8 (March 1963): 9–11.

"As Much Truth as One Can Bear." *The New York Times Book Review*, 14 January 1962, p. 1.

"At the Root of the Negro Problem." *Time*, 17 May 1963, pp. 26–27.

"Baldwin Excoriates Church for Hypocritical Stance." *Afro-American*, 16 July 1968.

"Battle Hymn." *New Leader* 30 (29 November 1947): 10.

"Bright World Darkened." *New Leader* 31 (24 January 1948): 11.

"Charge Within a Channel." *New Leader* 31 (24 April 1948): 11.

"Color." *Esquire* 58 (December 1962): 225.

"The Creative Dilemma: 'The War of an Artist with His Society Is a Lover's War.'" *Saturday Review* 57 (8 February 1964): 14–15.

"The Creative Process." In *Creative America*, edited by the National Cultural Center, pp. 17–21. New York: Ridge Press, 1962.

"The Crusade of Indignation." *Nation* 183 (7 July 1956): 18–22.

"The Dangerous Road before Martin Luther King." *Harper's* 222 (February 1961): 33–42.

"Dead Hand of Caldwell." *New Leader* 30 (6 December 1947): 10.

"Dear Sister." *Manchester Guardian Weekly*, 27 December 1970, p. 31.

"From Dreams of Love to Dreams of Terror." In *Natural Enemies? Youth and the Clash of Generations*, edited by Alexander Klein, pp. 274–79. Philadelphia: J. B. Lippincott, 1969.

"God's Country." *The New York Review of Books* 8 (23 March 1967): 20.

"The Harlem Ghetto: Winter 1948." *Commentary* 5 (February 1948): 165–70.

"The Image of the Negro." *Commentary* 5 (April 1948): 378–80.

"In Search of a Basis for Mutual Understanding and Racial Harmony." In *The Nature of Humane Society,* edited by H. Ober Hesse, pp. 231–40. Philadelphia: Fortress Press, 1976.

"James Baldwin on the Negro Actor." In *Anthology of the American Negro in the Theatre,* edited by Lindsay Patterson, pp. 127–30. New York: Publishers Company, 1967.

"Letters from a Journey." *Harper's* 226 (May 1963): 48–52.

"A Letter to Americans." *Freedomways* 8 (Spring 1968): 112–16.

"Literary Grab Bag." *New Leader* 31 (28 February 1948): 11.

"Lockridge: 'The American Myth.'" *New Leader* 31 (10 April 1948): 10.

"Mass Culture and the Creative Artist: Some Personal Notes." *Daedalus* 89 (Spring 1960): 373–76.

"Maxim Gorki as Artist." *Nation* 164 (12 April 1947): 427–28.

"Modern River Boys." *New Leader* 31 (14 August 1948): 12.

"The Negro at Home and Abroad." *Reporter* 5 (27 November 1951): 36–37.

"Negroes Are Anti-Semitic Because They're Anti-White." *New York Times Magazine,* 9 April 1967, p. 26.

"The New Lost Generation." *Esquire* 56 (July 1961): 113–15.

"The Nigger We Invent." *Integrated Education* 7 (March–April 1969): 15–23.

"On an Author: Excerpts from Letters." *New York Herald Tribune Book Review* 29 (31 May 1953): 3.

"On Catfish Row: Porgy and Bess in the Movies." *Commentary* 28 (September 1959): 246–48.

"An Open Letter to My Sister, Miss Angela Davis." *The New York Times,* 7 January 1971, p. 15.

"Paris Letter: A Question of Identity." *Partisan Review* 21 (July–August 1954): 402–10.

"Present and Future." *New Leader* 31 (13 March 1948): 11.

"Preservation of Innocence." *Zero* 1 (Summer 1949): 14–22.

"A Report from Occupied Territory." *Nation* 203 (11 July 1966): 39–43.

"Roots: The Saga of an American Family." *Unique* 1 (1976): 31–32.

"Sermons and Blues." *New York Times Book Review,* 29 March 1959, p. 6.

"Sidney Poitier." *Look* 32 (23 July 1968): 50–58.

"Smaller than Life." *Nation* 165 (19 July 1947): 78–79.

"Sweet Lorraine." *Esquire* 122 (November 1969): 139–40.

"A Talk to Harlem Teachers." In *Harlem, U.S.A.,* edited by John Henrik Clarke, pp. 171–80. New York: Collier Books, 1971.

"Talk to Teachers." *Saturday Review* 46 (21 December 1963): 42–44.

"Theatre: The Negro In and Out." *Negro Digest* 15 (October 1966): 37–44.

"There's a Bill Due That Has to Be Paid." *Life* 54 (24 May 1963): 81–84.

"They Can't Turn Back." *Mademoiselle* 51 (August 1960): 324.

"They Will Wait No More." *Negro Digest* 10 (July 1961): 77–82.

"Too Late, Too Late." *Commentary* 7 (January 1949): 96–99.
"Two Protests against Protest." *Perspectives USA* 2 (Winter 1953): 89–100.
"The Uses of the Blues." *Playboy* 11 (January 1964): 131.
"The War Crimes Tribunal." *Freedomways* 7 (Summer 1967): 242–44.
"We Can Change the Country." *Liberation* 8 (October 1963): 7–8.
Baldwin, James, et al. "What Kind of Men Cry?" *Ebony* 20 (June 1965): 47.
"What Price Freedom?" *Freedomways* 4 (Spring 1964): 191–95.
"When the War Hit Brownsville." *New Leader* 30 (17 May 1947): 12.
"The White Man's Guilt." *Ebony* 20 (August 1964): 47–48.
"White Racism or World Community?" *Ecumenical Review* 20 (October 1968): 371–76.
"Why a Stokely?" *St. Petersburg Times*, 3 March 1968, p. 1D.
"Without Grisly Gaiety." *New Leader* 30 (20 September 1947): 12.
"A Word from Writer Directly to Reader." In *Fiction of the Fifties* edited by Herbert Gold, pp. 18–19. New York: Doubleday, 1959.

II. Works on Baldwin

Criticism

Abramson, Doris E. *Negro Playwrights in American Theatre, 1925–1959.* New York: Columbia University Press, 1969.
Adams, Donald J. "Speaking of Books." *New York Times Book Review*, 28 January 1962, p. 2.
Adelsen, Charles E. "A Love Affair: James Baldwin and Istanbul." *Ebony* 25 (March 1970): 40–46.
Alexander, Charlotte A. *Baldwin's "Go Tell It on the Mountain," "Another Country," and Other Works: A Critical Commentary.* New York: Monarch Press, 1968.
———. "The 'Stink of Reality': Mothers and Whores in James Baldwin's Fiction." *Literature and Psychology* 18 (1968): 9–28.
Allen, Shirley S. "Religion Symbolism and Psychic Reality in Baldwin's *Go Tell It on the Mountain.*" *College Language Association Journal* 19 (December 1975): 173–99.
Anderson, Jervis. "Race, Rage and Eldridge Cleaver." *Commentary* 46 (December 1968): 63–69.
Arana, Gregorio. "The Baffling Creator—A Study of the Writing of James Baldwin." *Caribbean Quarterly* 12 (September 1966): 3–23.
Baker, Houston A., Jr. "The Embattled Craftsman: An Essay on James Baldwin." *Journal of African-Afro-American Affairs* 1 (1977): 28–51.
———. *Long Black Song: Essays in Black American Literature and Culture.* Charlottesville: University Press of Virginia, 1972.
"Baldwin: Gray Flannel Muslim?" *Christian Century* 80 (12 June 1963): 791.
"Baldwin Hits Mallory Case." *Muhammad Speaks*, 31 January 1964, p. 2.

Balliett, Whitney. "Wrong Pulpit." *New Yorker* 38 (4 August 1962): 69–71.

Bannett, William. "Weight of the City." *Atlantic* 210 (July 1962): 110–11.

Bannon, Barbara A. "How Margaret Mead and James Baldwin Got Together for *A Rap on Race.*" *Publishers Weekly* 199 (31 May 1971): 104–5.

Banta, Thomas J. "James Baldwin's Discovery of Identity." *Mawazo* 2 (June 1969): 33–41.

Bardeen, Constance L. "Love and Hate: Review of *Another Country.*" *Crisis* 69 (November 1962): 567–68.

Barksdale, Richard K. "Alienation and the Anti-Hero in Recent American Fiction." *College Language Association Journal* 10 (September 1966): 1–10.

———. "Temple of the Fire Baptized." *Phylon* 14 (Third quarter 1953): 326–27.

———, and Kinnamon, Keneth. *Black Writers of America: A Comprehensive Anthology.* New York: Macmillan Co., 1972.

Barr, Donald. "Guilt Was Everywhere." *New York Times Book Review,* 17 May 1953, p. 5.

Barrett, William. "Reader's Choice." *Atlantic Monthly* 206 (March 1963): 156.

Bell, George E. "The Dilemma of Love in *Go Tell It on the Mountain* and *Giovanni's Room.*" *College Language Association* 17 (March 1974): 397–406.

Berry, Boyd M. "Another Man Done Gone: Self-Pity in Baldwin's *Another Country.*" *Michigan Quarterly Review* 5 (Fall 1966): 285–90.

Bigsby, C. W. E., ed. *The American Writer.* 2 vols. Baltimore: Penguin Books, 1971.

———. "The Committed Writer: James Baldwin as Dramatist." *Twentieth Century Literature* 13 (April 1967): 39–48.

———. "Faith in the Power of Love." *Manchester Guardian Weekly,* 29 June 1974, p. 22.

Bingham, Robert K. "Two American Writers: I. Baldwin." *Reporter* 8 (23 June 1953): 38–39.

Binn, Sheldon. "Books of the Times." *New York Times,* 31 January 1963, p. 7.

"Black Man's Burden." *Times Literary Supplement,* 6 September 1963, p. 672.

Blaisdel, Gus. "A Literary Assessment: James Baldwin, the Writer." *Negro Digest* 13 (January 1964): 61–68.

Bloomfield, Caroline. "Religion and Alienation in James Baldwin, Bernard Malamud, and James F. Powers." *Religious Education* 57 (March–April 1962): 97–102.

Blount, Trevor. "A Slight Error in Continuity in James Baldwin's *Another Country.*" *Notes and Queries* 13 (March 1966): 102–3.

Bluefarb, Sam. "James Baldwin's 'Previous Condition'": A Problem of Identification." *Negro American Literature Forum* 3 (Spring 1969): 26–29.

Bond, Jean Carey. "The Fire Next Time." *Freedomways* (Spring 1963): 235–37.

Bone, Robert A. *The Negro Novel in America.* New Haven: Yale University Press, 1965.

————. "The Novels of James Baldwin." *Triquarterly* 2 (Winter 1965): 3–20.

Bonosky, Phillip. "The Negro Writer and Commitment." *Mainstream* 15 (February 1962): 16–22.

Boyle, Kay. "Introducing James Baldwin." In *Contemporary American Novelists*, edited by Harry T. Moore, pp. 155–57. Carbondale: Southern Illinois University Press, 1964.

Bradford, Melvin E. "Faulkner, James Baldwin, and the South." *Georgia Review* 20 (Winter 1966): 431–43.

Breit, Harvey. "James Baldwin and Two Footnotes." In *The Creative Present: Notes on Contemporary American Fiction*, edited by Nona Balakian and Charles Simmons, pp. 1–23. Garden City, New York: Doubleday and Co., 1967.

Brooks, Hallie B. "Baldwin in Paperback." *Phylon* 21 (Third Quarter 1960): 296–97.

Brown, Sterling A. "A Century of Negro Portraiture in American Literature." *Massachusetts Review* 7 (Winter 1966): 73–96.

Brudnoy, David. "Blues for Mr. Baldwin." *National Review* 24 (7 July 1972): 750–51.

Brustein, Robert. "Everybody Knows My Name." *New York Review of Books* 3 (17 December 1964): 10–11.

————. "Everybody's Protest Play." *New Republic* 150 (16 May 1964): 35–37.

Bryden, E. "Blues for Mister Charlie." *Partisan Review* 31 (September 1964): 389–94.

Buckley, William F., Jr. "Call to Color Blindness." *National Review* 14 (18 June 1963): 488.

————. "The Negro and the American Dream." *National Review* 17 (6 April 1965): 273.

Burks, Mary Fair. "James Baldwin's Protest Novel: *If Beale Street Could Talk*." *Negro American Literature Forum* 10 (Fall 1976): 83–87.

Butcher, Margaret J. *The Negro in American Culture*. New York: Alfred A. Knopf, 1956.

Butterfield, Stephen. *Black Autobiography in America*. Amherst: University of Massachusetts Press, 1974.

Byerman, K. E. "Words and Music: Narrative Ambiguity in Sonny's Blues." *Studies in Short Fiction* 19 (Fall 1982): 367–72.

Campbell, Finley. "More Notes of a Native Son." *Phylon* 23 (Spring 1962): 96–97.

Cartey, Wilfred. "I've Been Reading: The Realities of Four Negro Writers." *Columbia University Forum* 9 (Summer 1966): 34–42.

Cassidy, T. E. "The Long Struggle." *Commonweal* 58 (22 May 1953): 186.

Chamet, Jules, and Kaplan, Sidney. *Black and White in American Culture*. Amherst: University of Massachusetts Press, 1969.

Charney, Maurice. "James Baldwin's Quarrel with Richard Wright." *American Quarterly* 15 (Spring 1963): 65–75.

Clark, Michael. "James Baldwin's Sonny's Blues: Childhood, Light, and Art." *College Language Association Journal* 29 (December 1985): 197–205.

Clarke, John Henrik. "The Alienation of James Baldwin." *Journal of Human Relations* 12 (First quarter 1964): 65–75.

———. "The Origin and Growth of Afro-American Literature." *Negro Digest* (December 1967): 54–67.

Cleaver, Eldridge. *Soul on Ice.* New York: McGraw-Hill, 1968.

Cohn, Ruby. *Dialogue in American Drama.* Bloomington: Indiana University Press, 1971.

Coles, Robert. "Baldwin's Burden." *Partisan Review* 31 (Summer 1964): 409–16.

———. "James Baldwin Back Home." *New York Times Book Review,* 31 July 1977, p. 1.

Collier, Eugenia W. "The Phrase Unbearably Repeated." *Phylon* 25 (Fall 1964): 288–96.

———. "Thematic Patterns in Baldwin's Essays: A Study in Chaos." *Black World* 21 (June 1972): 28–34.

Cook, Bruce. "Writers in Midstream: John Williams and James Baldwin." *Critic* 21 (February–March 1963): 35–40.

Coombs, Orde. "The Devil Finds Work." *New York Times Book Review,* 2 May 1976, pp. 6–7.

Corona, Mario. "La Saggistica di James Baldwin." *Studi Americani* 15 (1969): 433–63.

Cox, C. B., and Jones, A. R. "After the Tranquilized Fifties: Notes on Sylvia Plath and James Baldwin." *Critical Quarterly* 6 (Summer 1964): 107–22.

Cruttwell, Patrick. "Fiction Chronicle." *Hudson Review* 15 (Winter 1962): 593–98.

Curley, Thomas F. "The Quarrel with Time in American Fiction." *American Scholar* 29 (Autumn 1960): 558.

Curling, Maud. "James Baldwin y la iglesia negra norteamericana en la novela *Go Tell It on the Mountain.*" *Revista Un Costa Rica* 34 (1972): 87–95.

Dance, Daryl C. "You Can't Go Home Again: James Baldwin and the South." *College Language Association Journal* 18 (September 1974): 81–90.

Dane, Peter. "Baldwin's Other Country." *Transition* 5 (1966): 38–40.

Daniels, Mark R. "Estrangement, Betrayal, and Atonement: The Political Theory of James Baldwin." *Studies in Black Literature* 7 (Autumn 1976): 10–13.

Davis, Arthur P., *From the Dark Tower: Afro-American Writers, 1900–1960.* Washington, D.C.: Howard University Press, 1974.

Davis, Arthur P., and Redding, Saunders J. *Cavalcade: Negro American Writing from 1760 to the Present.* Boston: Houghton Mifflin, 1971.

DeMott, Benjamin. "James Baldwin on the Sixties: Acts and Revelations." *Saturday Review* 55 (27 May 1972): 63–66.

Dickstein, Morris. "Wright, Baldwin, Cleaver." *New Letters* 38 (Winter 1971): 117–24.

Donald, David. "A Fascinating Book." *Virginia Quarterly Review* 47 (Autumn 1971): 619–22.

Donlan, Dan. "Cleaver on Baldwin and Wright." *Clearing House* 48 (April 1974): 508–9.

Donoghue, Denis. "Blues for Mr. Baldwin." *New York Review of Books* 5 (9 December 1965): 6–7.

Driver, Tom F. *"Blues for Mr. Charlie; The Review That Was Too True To Be Published."* *Negro Digest* 13 (September 1964): 34–40.

Dupree, F. W. *The King of the Cats and Other Remarks on Writers and Writing.* New York: Farrar, Straus, and Giroux, 1965.

Eckman, Fern Marja. *The Furious Passage of James Baldwin.* New York: M. Evans and Co., 1966.

Elkoff, Marvin. "Everybody Knows His Name." *Esquire* 62 (August 1964): 59–64.

Ellison, Ralph. "The World and the Jug." *New Leader* 46 (9 December 1963): 22–26.

———. "The Writer and the Critic—An Exchange: A Rejoinder." *New Leader* 47 (3 February 1964): 15–22.

Emanuel, James A. "James Baldwin." In *Contemporary Novelists,* edited by James Vinson, pp. 82–86. New York: St. Martin's Press, 1976.

———, and Gross, Theodore L. *Dark Symphony: Negro Literature in America.* New York: Free Press, 1968.

Ethredge, James M., and Kopala, Barbara, eds. *Contemporary Authors.* Detroit: Gale Research Co., 1963.

Evanier, David. "The Identity of James Baldwin." *Commonweal* 77 (28 December 1962): 365.

Fabre, Michel. "Père et fils dans *Go Tell It on the Mountain* de James Baldwin." *Etudes Anglaises* 23 (January–March 1970): 47–61.

———. *The Unfinished Quest of Richard Wright.* Translated by Isabel Barzun. New York: William Morrow, 1973.

Featherstone, Joseph. "Blues for Mr. Baldwin." *New Republic* 153 (27 November 1965): 34–36.

Fiedler, Leslie A. "A Homosexual Dilemma." *New Leader* 39 (10 December 1956): 16–17.

Finkelstein, S. W. *Existentialism and Alienation in American Literature.* New York: International Publishers, 1965.

Finn, James. "The Author Replies." *Commonweal* 77 (28 December 1962): 365–66.

———. "The Identity of James Baldwin." *Commonweal* 77 (26 October 1962): 172–74.

———. "James Baldwin's Vision." *Commonweal* 78 (26 July 1963): 447–49.

Fleischauer, John F. "James Baldwin's Style." *College Composition and Communication* 26 (March 1975): 141–48.

Flint, Robert W. "The Undying Apocalypse." *Partisan Review* 24 (Winter 1957): 139–45.

Fontinell, Eugene. "The Identity of James Baldwin." *Interracial Review* 35 (September 1962): 194–99.

Foote, Dorothy. "James Baldwin's 'Holler Books.'" *CEA Critic* 25 (May 1963): 8.

Ford, Nick Aaron. "The Fire Next Time? A Critical Survey of Belles-Lettres by and about Negroes Published in 1963." *Phylon* 25 (Summer 1964): 123–34.

———. "Search for Identity: A Critical Survey of Significant Belles-Lettres by and about Negroes Published in 1961." *Phylon* 23 (Summer 1962): 128–30.

———. "Walls Do a Prison Make: A Critical Survey of Significant Belles-Lettres by and about Negroes Published in 1962." *Phylon* 24 (Summer 1963): 123–34.

Forman, Enid G. *Put Me in Print: A Story of James Baldwin.* Washington, D.C., n.d.

Foster, David E. "'Cause My House Fell Down: The Theme of the Fall in Baldwin's Novels." *Critique: Studies in Modern Fiction* 13 (1971): 50–62.

Friedenberg, Edgar Z. "Another Country for an Arkansas Traveler." *New Republic* 147 (27 August 1962): 23–26.

Friedman, Neil. "James Baldwin and Psychotherapy." *Psychotherapy* 3 (November 1966): 177–83.

Fryer, Sarah. "Retreat from Experience: Despair and Suicide in James Baldwin's Novels." *The Journal of the Midwest Modern Language Association* 19 (Spring 1986): 21–28.

Fulford, Robert. "On Books: The Black Nationalism of the New James Baldwin." *Maclean's Review* 76 (27 July 1963): 45–46.

Gayle, Addison, Jr. "A Defense of James Baldwin." *College Language Association Journal* 10 (March 1967): 201–8.

———. "The Dialectic of *The Fire Next Time.*" *Negro History Bulletin* 30 (April 1967): 15–16.

———. "Perhaps Not So Soon One Morning." *Phylon* 29 (Winter 1968): 396–402.

Gerard, Albert. "James Baldwin et la Religiosité Noire." *Revue Nouvelle* 33 (February 1961): 177–86.

———. "Humanism and Negritude: Notes on the Contemporary Afro-American Novel." *Diogenes* 37 (Spring 1962): 115–33.

Gibson, Donald B., ed. *Five Black Writers: Essays on Wright, Ellison, Baldwin, Hughes, and Leroi Jones.* New York: New York University Press, 1970.

———. "The Politics of Ellison and Baldwin." In *The Politics of Twentieth-*

Century Writers, edited by George Panishas, pp. 307–20. New York: Hawthorne Publishing Co., 1971.
———. "Wright's Invisible Native Son." *American Quarterly* 21 (Winter 1969): 728–38.
Giles, J. R. "Religious Alienation and 'Homosexual Consciousness' in *City of Night* and *Go Tell It on the Mountain.*" *College English* 36 (November 1974): 369–80.
Golden, Harry. "A Comment on James Baldwin's Letter." *Crisis* 70 (March 1963): 145–46.
Goldman, Suzy B. "James Baldwin's 'Sonny's Blues': A Message in Music." *Negro American Literature Forum* 8 (Fall 1974): 231–33.
Goodman, Paul. "Not Enough of a World to Grow in." *New York Times Book Review,* 24 June 1962, p. 5.
Gounard, Jean-François. "La Carrière Singulière de James Baldwin: 1924–1970." *Revue de l'Université d'Ottawa* 44 (December 1974): 507–18.
———. "L'Avenir de James Baldwin." *Europe* 578 (June–July 1977): 186–97.
Graves, J. "Disorganization Men." *New Statesman* 65 (8 February 1963): 202–4.
Graves, Wallace. "The Question of Moral Energy in James Baldwin's *Go Tell It on the Mountain.*" *College Language Association Journal* 7 (March 1964): 215–23.
Gresset, Michel. "Sur James Baldwin." *Mercure de France* 350 (April 1964): 653–55.
Gross, Barry. "The 'Uninhabitable Darkness' of Baldwin's *Another Country*: Image and Theme." *Negro American Literature Forum* 6 (Winter 1972): 113–21.
Gross, Seymour Lee, ed. *Images of the Negro in American Literature.* Chicago: University of Chicago Press, 1966.
Gross, Theodore L. *The Heroic Ideal in American Literature.* New York: The Free Press, 1971.
———. "The World of James Baldwin." *Critique* 7 (Winter 1964): 139–49.
Hagopian, John V. "James Baldwin: The Black and the Red-White-and-Blue." *College Language Association Journal* 7 (December 1963): 133–40.
Hardwick, Elizabeth. "All about Love." *Harper's* 225 (July 1962): 90–92.
Harper, Howard M., Jr. *Desperate Faith: A Study of Bellow, Salinger, Mailer, Baldwin, and Updike.* Chapel Hill: University of North Carolina Press, 1967.
Harris, Trudier. *Black Women in the Fiction of James Baldwin.* Knoxville: University of Tennessee, 1985.
Heermance, J. Noel. "A White Critic's Viewpoint: The Modern Negro Novel." *Negro Digest* 13 (May 1964): 66–76.
Heiberg, Inger. "James Baldwin—Negerforfatter og Dikter.' *Samtiden* 73 (May 1965): 280–87.

Hentoff, Nat. "Baldwin and His Critics." *Village Voice,* 2 August 1962, p. 6.
————. "It's Terrifying." *New York Herald Tribune Books,* 16 June 1963, p. 1.
————. "Uninventing the Negro." *Evergreen Review* 9 (November 1965): 34–36.
Hernton, Calvin C. "Blood of the Lamb: The Ordeal of James Baldwin." In *Amistad I: Writings on Black History and Culture,* edited by John A. Williams and Charles F. Harris, pp. 183–225. New York: Random House, 1970.
————. *White Papers for White Americans.* New York: Doubleday Co., 1966.
Hicks, Granville. "A Gun in the Hand of a Hater." *Saturday Review* 47 (2 May 1964): 27–28.
Hill, Herbert, ed. *Anger and Beyond: The Negro Writer in the United States.* New York: Harper and Row, 1966.
Hoffman, Stanton. "The Cities of the Night: John Rechy's *City of Night* and the American Literature of Homosexuality." *Chicago Review* 17 (1964): 195–202.
————. *The Modern Novel in America.* Chicago: Henry Regnery Co., 1963.
Howard, Jane. "Doom and Glory of Knowing Who You Are." *Life* 104 (24 May 1963).
Howe, Irving. "Black Boys and Native Sons." *Dissent* 10 (Autumn 1963): 353–68.
————. "James Baldwin: At Ease in Apocalypse." *Harper's* 237 (September 1968): 92–100.
————. "A Protest of His Own." *New York Times Book Review,* 2 July 1961, p. 4.
————. "The Writer and the Critic—An Exchange: A Reply to Ralph Ellison." *New Leader* 47 (3 February 1963): 12–14.
Hughes, Langston. "From Harlem to Paris." *New York Times Book Review,* 26 February 1956, p. 26.
Inge, M. Thomas. "James Baldwin's Blues." *Notes on Contemporary Literature* 2 (September 1972): 8–11.
Isaacs, Harold R. "Five Writers and Their African Ancestors." *Phylon* 21 (Winter 1960): 322–29.
Ivy, James W. "The Fairie Queenes." *Crisis* 64 (February 1957): 123.
————. "Book Reviews: Nobody Knows My Name." *Crisis* 68 (October 1961): 522.
Jacobson, Daniel. "James Baldwin as Spokesman." *Commentary* 32 (December 1961): 497–502.
"James Baldwin." In *Current Biography Yearbook, 1964,* edited by Charles Moritz, pp. 22–24. New York: H. W. Wilson, 1964.
Jarrett, Thomas D. "Search for Identity." *Phylon* 17 (First Quarter 1956): 87–88.
Jones, B. F. "James Baldwin: The Struggle for Identity." *The British Journal of Sociology* 17 (June 1966): 107–21.

Jones, Leroi. *Home: Social Essays*. New York: William Morrow, 1966.

Jordan, Jennifer. "Cleaver vs. Baldwin: Icing the White Negro." *Black Books Bulletin* 1 (Winter 1972): 12–15.

Kattan, Naim. "Deux Ecrivains Americains." *Ecrits du Canada Français* 17 (1964): 87–135.

Kauffman, Stanley. "Another Baldwin." *New York Times Book Review*, 12 December 1965, p. 5.

Kazin, Alfred. *Contemporaries*. Boston: Little, Brown, and Co., 1962.

"Kennedy and Baldwin: The Gulf." *Newsweek*, 3 June 1963, p. 19.

Kent, George E. "Baldwin and the Problem of Being." *College Language Association Journal* 7 (March 1964): 202–14.

Kim, Kichung. "Wright, the Protest Novel, and Baldwin's Faith." *College Language Association Journal* 17 (March 1974): 387–96.

Kinnamon, Keneth, ed. *James Baldwin: A Collection of Critical Essays*. Englewood Cliffs, N.J.: Prentice-Hall, 1974.

Klein, Marcus. *After Alienation: American Novels in Mid-Century*. New York: World Publishing Co., 1962.

Langer, Lawrence. "To Make Freedom Real: James Baldwin and the Conscience of America." *Americana-Austriaca* 58 (1966): 217–28.

Larry 5X, "Baldwin 'Baptised' in Fire This Time." *Muhammad Speaks*, 23 February 1973, p. 25.

Lash, John. "Baldwin Beside Himself: A Study of Modern Phallicism." *College Language Association Journal* 8 (December 1964): 132–40.

Leaks, Sylvester. "James Baldwin—I Know His Name." *Freedomways* 3 (Winter 1963): 102–5.

Lee, Brian. "James Baldwin: Caliban to Prospero." In *The Black American Writer*, edited by C. W. E. Bigsby, Vol. 1, pp. 167–79. Baltimore: Penguin Books, 1971.

Lee, Robert A. "James Baldwin and Matthew Arnold: Thoughts on 'Relevance.'" *College Language Association Journal* 14 (March 1971): 324–30.

Lester, J. "Some Tickets Are Better: The Mixed Achievement of James Baldwin." *Dissent* 33 (Spring 1986): 189–92.

Levant, Howard. "Aspiraling We Should Go." *Midcontinent American Studies Journal* 4 (Fall 1963): 2–20.

Levin, David. "James Baldwin's Autobiographical Essays: The Problem of Negro Identity." *Massachusetts Review* 5 (Winter 1964): 239–47.

Lewis, Theophilus. "Blues for Mr. Charlie." *America* 110 (30 May 1964): 776–77.

Littlejohn, David. *Black on White: A Critical Survey of Writings by American Negroes*. New York: Grossman, 1966.

———. "Exemplary and Other Baldwins." *Nation* 13 (13 December 1965): 478–80.

Llorens, David. "Books Noted." *Black World* 17 (August 1968): 51.

Long, R. E. "From Elegant to Hip." *Nation* 206 (10 June 1968): 769–70.

Long, Robert Emmet. "Love and Wrath in the Fiction of James Baldwin." *English Record* 19 (February 1969): 50–57.

Luce, Phillip A. "Communications on James Baldwin." *Mainstream* 15 (May 1962): 45–48.

Macebuh, Stanley. *James Baldwin: A Critical Study*. New York: Joseph Okpaku Publishing Co., 1973.

MacInnes, Colin. "Dark Angel: The Writings of James Baldwin." *Encounter* 21 (August 1963): 22–33.

Mailer, Norman. "Norman Mailer vs. Nine Writers." *Esquire* 60 (July 1963): 63–69.

Major, Clarence. *The Dark and Feeling: Black American Writers and Their Work*. New York: Joseph Okpaku Publishing Co., 1974.

Malcolm, Donald. "Books: The Author in Search of Himself." *New Yorker* 37 (25 November 1961): 233–38.

Marcus, Steven. "The American Negro in Search of Identity." *Commentary* 16 (November 1963): 456–63.

Margolies, Edward. *Native Sons: A Critical Study of Twentieth-Century Negro American Authors*. New York: J. B. Lippincott Co., 1968.

May, John R. *Toward a New Earth: Apocalypse in the American Novel*. Notre Dame, Ind.: University of Notre Dame Press, 1972.

Mayfield, Julian. "And Then Came Baldwin." *Freedomways* 3 (Spring 1963): 143–55.

Mead, Margaret. "A Rap on Race: How James Baldwin and I Talked a Book." *Redbook* 137 (September 1971): 70–75.

Mergen, Bernard. "James Baldwin and the American Conundrum." *Moderna Sprak* 57 (December 1963): 397–405.

Meriwether, L. M. "Broadway Hit for Baldwin: The Amen Corner." *Negro Digest* 14 (January 1965): 40–47.

———. "James Baldwin: Fiery Voice of the Negro Revolt." *Negro Digest* 12 (August 1963): 3–7.

Meserve, Walter. "James Baldwin's 'Agony Way.'" In *The Black American Writer*, edited by C. W. E. Bigsby, Vol. 2, pp. 171–86. Baltimore: Penguin Books, 1971.

Mitchell, Lofton. *Black Drama*. New York: Hawthorn Books, 1967.

Mitra, B. D. "The Wright-Baldwin Controversy." *Indian Journal of American Studies* 1 (1969): 101–5.

Moller, Karin. "James Baldwin's Theme of 'Identity' and His 'Fall' Metaphor." *Essays in Criticism* 2 (March 1974): 34–50.

———. *The Theme of Identity in the Essays of James Baldwin: An Interpretation*. Göteborg, Sweden: Acta Universitatis Gothoburgensis, 1975.

Moon, Eric. "Biography—Personal Narrative." *Library Journal* 86 (June 1961): 2792.

Moore, John Rees. "An Embarrassment of Riches: Baldwin's *Going to Meet the Man*." *Hollins Critic* 2 (December 1965): 1–12.

Mootry, M. K. "Baldwin's *Go Tell It on the Mountain*." *Explicator* 43 (Winter 1985): 50–52.

Morrison, Allan. "The Angriest Young Man." *Ebony* 16 (October 1961): 23–30.

———. "James Baldwin, Protest Fiction and the Blues Tradition." In *The Omni-Americans*, edited by Albert Murray, pp. 142–68. New York: Outerbridge and Dienstfrey, 1970.

Mosher, M. "James Baldwin's Blues." *College Language Association Journal* 26 (Spring 1982): 112–24.

Mowe, Gregory, and Nobles, W. Scott. "James Baldwin's Message for White America." *Quarterly Journal of Speech* 58 (April 1972): 142–51.

Murray, Albert. *The Omni-Americans: New Perspectives on Black Experience and American Culture*. New York: Outerbridge and Dienstfrey, 1970.

Murray, Donald C. "James Baldwin's 'Sonny's Blues': Complicated and Simple." *Studies in Short Fiction* 14 (Fall 1977): 353–57.

Newman, Charles. "The Lesson of the Master: Henry James and James Baldwin." *Yale Review* 56 (October 1966): 45–59.

Nichols, Charles H. "James Baldwin: A Skillful Executioner." *Studies on the Left* 2 (Winter 1963): 74–79.

Noble, David. *The Eternal Adam and the New World Garden*. New York: George Braziller, 1968.

Nyren, Dorothy, ed. *A Library of Literary Criticism*. New York: Frederick Ungar Publishing Co., 1961.

Oates, Joyce Carol. "A Quite Moving and Very Traditional Celebration of Love: *If Beale Street Could Talk*." *New York Times Book Review*, 26 May 1974, pp. 1–2.

O'Daniel, Therman B., ed. *James Baldwin: A Critical Evaluation*. Washington, D.C.: Howard University Press, 1977.

———. "James Baldwin: An Interpretive Study." *College Language Association Journal* 7 (September 1963): 37–47.

Ognibene, Elaine R. "Black Literature Revisited: 'Sonny's Blues.'" *English Journal* 60 (January 1971): 36–37.

Panichas, George, ed. *The Politics of Twentieth-Century Writers*. New York: Hawthorne Publishing Co., 1971.

Patterson, Orlando H. "The Essays of James Baldwin." *New Left Review* 26 (Summer 1964): 31–38.

Peterson, Fred. "James Baldwin and Eduardo Mallea: Two Essayists' Search for Identity." *Discourse* 10 (Winter 1967): 97–107.

Phillips, Louis. "The Novelist as Playwright: Baldwin, McCullers, and Bellow." In *Modern American Drama: Essays in Criticism*, edited by William W. Taylor, pp. 145–62. Deland, Fla.: Everett/Edwards, 1968.

"Playboy Interview: Huey Newton." *Playboy* 20 (May 1973): 84.

Ploski, Harry A., and Marr, Warren. *The Negro Almanac: A Reference Work on the Afro-American.* New York: Bellwether Publishing Co., 1976.

Plummer, Wayne. "Baldwin's Burden." *The Christian Century* 80 (28 August 1963): 1057.

Podhoretz, Norman. *Doings and Undoings: The Fifties and After in American Writing.* New York: Farrar, Straus, and Co., 1964.

Potter, Vilma. "Baldwin and Odets: The High Cost of 'Crossing.'" *California English Journal* 1 (Fall 1965): 17–41.

Powers, Lyall. "Henry James and James Baldwin: The Complex Figure." *Modern Fiction Studies* 30 (Winter 1984): 651–67.

Pratt, Louis Hill. *James Baldwin.* Boston: Twayne Publishers, 1978.

Raddatz, Fritz J. "Schwarz ist die Farbe der Einsamkeit: Skizze zu einer Porträt James Baldwin." *Frankfurter Hefte* 20 (1965): 44–52.

"Ralph Ellison Talks about James Baldwin." *Negro Digest* 11 (September 1962): 61.

Redding, J. Saunders. *The American Negro Writer and His Roots.* New York: American Society of African Culture, 1960.

———. "In His Native Land." *New York Herald Tribune Book Review,* 25 June 1961, p. 36.

———. "James Baldwin Miscellany." *New York Herald Tribune Book Review,* 26 February 1966, p. 4.

———. "Since Richard Wright." *African Forum* 1 (Spring 1966): 21–23.

Reilly, John M. "'Sonny's Blues': James Baldwin's Image of Black Community." *Negro American Literature Forum* 4 (July 1970): 56–60.

Rosenblatt, Roger. *Black Fiction.* Cambridge, Mass.: Harvard University Press, 1974.

Roth, Philip. "Channel X: Two Plays on the Race Conflict." *New York Review of Books* 2 (28 May 1964): 10–11.

Rubin, L. D. "The Great American Joke." *South Atlantic Quarterly* 72 (Winter 1973): 82–94.

Rupp, Richard H. *Celebration in Postwar American Fiction: 1945–1967.* Coral Gables, Fla.: University of Miami Press, 1970.

Sayre, Robert. "James Baldwin's *Other Country.*" In *Contemporary American Novelists,* edited by Harry T. Moore, pp. 158–69. Carbondale: Southern Illinois University Press, 1964.

Scheller, Bernard. "Die Gestalt des Farbingenbei Williams, Albee, und Baldwin und ihre Szenische Realisierung in DDR-Aufführungen." *Zeitschrift für Anglistik und Amerikanistik* 20 (1972): 137–57.

Schlesinger, Arthur M., Jr. *A Thousand Days: John F. Kennedy in the White House.* Boston: Houghton Mifflin, 1965.

Schrero, Elliot M. "*Another Country* and the Sense of Self." *Black Academy Review* 2 (Spring–Summer 1971): 91–100.

Schroth, Raymond A. "James Baldwin's Search." *Catholic World* 198 (February 1964): 288–94.

Schurer, Mark. *The Literature of America: Twentieth Century.* New York: McGraw-Hill, 1970.

Scott, Nathan A., Jr. "Judgment Marked by a Cellar: The American Negro Writer and the Dialectic of Despair." *Denver Quarterly* 2 (Summer 1967): 5–35.

Scott, Robert L. "Rhetoric, Black Power, and Baldwin's *Another Country.*" *Journal of Black Studies* 1 (September 1970): 21–34.

Sheed, Wilfred. *The Morning After: Selected Essays and Reviews.* New York: Farrar, Straus, and Giroux, 1971.

Silvera, Frank. "Towards a Theater of Understanding." *Negro Digest* 18 (April 1969): 33–35.

Simmons, Harvey G. "James Baldwin and the Negro Conundrum." *Antioch Review* 23 (Summer 1963): 250–55.

Smart, William. *Eight Modern Essayists.* New York: St. Martin's Press, 1965.

Southwick, Albert B. "James Baldwin's Jeremiad." *Christian Century* 82 (24 March 1965): 362–64.

Spector, Robert D. "Everybody Knows His Name." *New York Herald Tribune Book Review,* 17 June 1962, p. 2.

Spender, Stephen. "James Baldwin: Voice of a Revolution." *Partisan Review* 30 (Summer 1963): 256–60.

Spingarn, Arthur B. "Notes of a Native Son." *Crisis* 63 (February 1956): 87.

Standley, Fred L. "Another Country, Another Time." *Studies in the Novel* 4 (Fall 1972): 504–12.

———. "James Baldwin: The Artist as Incorrigible Disturber of the Peace." *Southern Humanities Review* 4 (Winter 1970): 18–30.

———. "James Baldwin: The Crucial Situation." *South Atlantic Quarterly* 65 (Summer 1966): 371–81.

Stanton, Robert. "Outrageous Fiction: Crime and Punishment and Native Son." *Pacific Coast Philology* 4 (April 1969): 52–58.

Steinem, Gloria. "James Baldwin, An Original: A Sharpened View of Him." *Vogue* 144 (July 1964): 78–79.

Straumann, Heinrich. *American Literature in the Twentieth Century.* 3rd rev. ed. New York: Harper and Row, 1965.

Strong, Augusta. "Note on James Baldwin." *Freedomways* 2 (Spring 1962): 167–71.

Strout, Cushing. "Uncle Tom's Cabin and the Portent of Millennium." *Yale Review* 57 (Spring 1968): 375–85.

Sylvander, Carolyn Wedin. *James Baldwin.* New York: Ungar, 1980.

Tedesco, J. L. "*Blues for Mister Charlie:* The Rhetorical Dimension." *Players* 50 (Fall–Winter): 20–23.

Thompson, John. "Baldwin: The Prophet as Artist." *Commentary* 45 (June 1968): 67–69.

Thompson, Thomas. "Magical Eleventh-Hour Save: *The Amen Corner.*" *Life* 106 (14 May 1965): 16.

Ulman, Ruth. "James Baldwin: Biographical Sketch." *Wilson Library Bulletin* 33 (February 1959): 392.

Van Sickle, Milton. "James Baldwin in Black and White." *Trace* 54 (Autumn 1964): 222–25.

Warren, Robert Penn. *Who Speaks for the Negro?* New York: Random House, 1965.

Watkins, Mel. "The Fire Next Time This Time." *New York Times Book Review,* 28 May 1972, pp. 17–18.

Watson, Edward A. "The Novels of James Baldwin: Case-Book of a Lover's War with the United States." *Queen's Quarterly* 72 (Summer 1965): 385–402.

Weathersby, W. J. *Squaring Off: Mailer vs. Baldwin.* New York: Mason/Charter, 1977.

Webster, Harvey C. "Community of Pride." *Saturday Review* 36 (16 May 1953): 14.

Werner, Craig. "The Economic Evolution of James Baldwin." *College Language Association Journal* 23 (September 1979): 12–31.

Wills, Anthony. "The Use of Coincidence in 'Notes of a Native Son.'" *Negro American Literature Forum* 8 (Fall 1974): 234–35.

Wills, Gary. "What Color is God?" *National Review* 14 (21 May 1963): 408–17.

Winslow, Henry F. "Church Sermon." *Crisis* 60 (December 1953): 637–38.

Wustenhagen, Heinz. "James Baldwin's Essays und Romane: Versuch einer ersten Einschatzung." *Zeitschrift für Anglistik und Amerikanistik* 13 (1965): 117–57.

Dissertations

Bayne, Barbara S. "The Role and Rhetoric of Female Characters in James Baldwin's Fiction." Ph.D. dissertation, Indiana University of Pennsylvania, 1983.

Bennett, Joanne S. "James Baldwin: A Contemporary Novelist of Manners." Ph.D. dissertation, Indiana University, 1974.

Breaux, Elwin E. "Comic Elements in Selected Prose Works by James Baldwin, Ralph Ellison, and Langston Hughes." Ph.D. dissertation, Oklahoma State University, 1972.

Britt, David. "The Image of the White Man in the Fiction of Langston Hughes, Richard Wright, James Baldwin, and Ralph Ellison." Ph.D. dissertation, Emory University, 1968.

Cowan, Kathryn Osburn. "Black/White Stereotypes in the Fiction of Richard Wright, James Baldwin, and Ralph Ellison." Ph.D. dissertation, St. Louis University, 1972.

Davis, Ursula B. "The Afro-American Musician and Writer in Paris during the 1950's and 1960's: A Study of Kenny Clarke, Donald Byrd, Chester Himes and James Baldwin." Ph.D. dissertation, University of Pittsburgh, 1983.

Ellison, Curtis W. "Black Adam: The Adamic Assertion and the Afro-American Novelist." Ph.D. dissertation, University of Minnesota, 1971.

Fisher, Lester Allen. "The Uses and Effects of Violence in the Fiction and Drama of James Baldwin." Ph.D. dissertation, Brown University, 1977.

Henderson, Mae G. "In Another Country: Afro-American Expatriate Novelists in France, 1946–1974." Ph.D. dissertation, Yale University, 1983.

Holloway, Clayton Glenn. "James Baldwin as a Writer of Short Fiction: An Evaluation." Ph.D. dissertation, Bowling Green State University, 1976.

Hughes, Joanne. "Elements of the Confessional Mode in the Novels of James Baldwin: 1954–1979." Ph.D. dissertation, Northern Illinois University, 1980.

Jackson, Edward Merica. "Fathers and Sons: An Analysis of the Writings of James Baldwin." Ph.D. dissertation, Syracuse University, 1975.

Jackson, Jacquelyn. "The Black Novelist and the Expatriate Experience: Richard Wright, James Baldwin, Chester Himes." Ph.D. dissertation, University of Kentucky, 1983.

Jackson, Jocelyn E. W. "The Problem of Identity in the Essays and Selected Novels of James Baldwin." Ph.D. dissertation, Emory University, 1973.

Korzus, Margaret G. "James Baldwin's Concept of the Artist and the Rebel: An Interpretation Based on Albert Camus and Otto Rank." Ph.D. dissertation, University of Denver, 1977.

Nelson, Emmanuel S. "Alienated Rebels: John Rechy and James Baldwin." Ph.D. dissertation, University of Tennessee, 1983.

Palosaari, Ronald G. "The Image of the Black Minister in the Black Novel from Dunbar to Baldwin." Ph.D. dissertation, University of Minnesota, 1970.

Reid, Kenneth R. "James Baldwin's Fiction: Literary Artistry in Special Pleading." Ph.D. dissertation, Kansas State University, 1972.

Smith, Cynthia Janis. "Escape and Quest in the Literature of Black Americans." Ph.D. dissertation, Yale University, 1975.

Thornton, Jerome E. "James Baldwin and the Christian Tradition." Ph.D. dissertation, State University of New York at Buffalo, 1977.

Van Heusen, Lawrence Lewis. "The Embodiment of Religious Meaning in the Works of James Baldwin." D.A. dissertation, State University of New York at Albany, 1980.

Zeitlow, Edward R. "Wright to Hansberry: The Evolution of Outlook in Four Negro Writers." Ph.D. dissertation, University of Washington, 1967.

Bibliographies

Adelman, Irving, and Dworkin, Rita. *The Contemporary Novel: A Checklist of Critical Literature on the British and American Novel Since 1945*. Metuchen, N.J.: Scarecrow Press, 1972.

Bobia, Rosa Mae Williamson. "James Baldwin and His Francophone Critics: An Analysis and Annotated Bibliography." Ph.D. dissertation, 1986.

Boyd, George N., and Boyd, Lois. *Religion in Contemporary Fiction: Criticism from 1945 to the Present*. San Antonio, Texas: Trinity University Press, 1973.

Breed, Paul F., and Sniderman, Florence. *Dramatic Criticism Index*. Detroit: Gale Research Co., 1972.

Corrigan, Robert A. "Afro-American Fiction: A Checklist, 1853–1970." *Midcontinent American Studies Journal* 11 (1970): 114–35.

Dance, Daryl C. "James Baldwin." In *Black American Writers: Bibliographical Essays*, edited by M. Thomas Inge, et al., pp. 73–120. New York: St. Martin's Press, 1978.

Fischer, Russell G. "James Baldwin: A Bibliography, 1947–1962." *Bulletin of Bibliography* 24 (January–April 1965): 127–30.

Jones, Mary E. "James Baldwin." Center for African and African-American Studies Bibliography, no. 5, mimeographed. Atlanta: Atlanta University, n.d.

Kindt, Kathleen A. "James Baldwin, A Checklist: 1947–1962" *Bulletin of Bibliography* 24 (January–April 1965): 124–36.

Leary, Lewis. *Articles on American Literature, 1950–1967*. Durham, N.C.: Duke University Press, 1970.

Mauro, Walter. *Baldwin*. Florence, Italy: La Nuova Italia, 1976.

Pownall, David. *Articles on Twentieth Century Literature: An Annotated Bibliography, 1954–1970*. New York: Kraus-Thomson Organization Ltd., 1973.

Rosa, Alfred F., and Eschholz, eds. *Contemporary Fiction in America and England, 1950–1970: A Guide to Information Services*. Detroit: Gale Research Co., 1976.

Rush, Theressa Gunnels, et al. *Black American Writers: A Biographical and Bibliographical Dictionary*. Metuchen, N.J.: Scarecrow Press, 1975.

Sader, Marion, ed. *Comprehensive Index to English Language Magazines, 1890–1970*. Millwood, N.Y.: Kraus-Thomson Organization Ltd., 1976.

Standley, Fred L. "James Baldwin: A Checklist, 1963–67." *Bulletin of Bibliography* 25 (May–August 1968): 135.

———, and Standley, Nancy V. *James Baldwin: A Reference Guide*. Boston: G. K. Hall and Co., 1980.

Turner, Darwin T. *Afro-American Writers*. New York: Appleton-Century-Crofts, 1970.

Obituaries and Tributes

Angelou, Maya; Morrison, Toni; Baraka, Amiri; Styron, William. "James Baldwin: His Voice Remembered." *New York Times Book Review,* December 20, 1987, p. 1.

Barnes, Bart. "James Baldwin, Playwright, Novelist, Dies." *Washington Post,* December 2, 1987, p. A1.

Bruning, Fred. "The Empty Shoes of a Native Son." *Maclean's* 100 (December 1987): 13.

Daniels, Lee A. "Baldwin is Eulogized as a Mentor, Writer, Social Catalyst and Friend." *New York Times,* December 9, 1987, p. 53.

Daniels, Lee A. "James Baldwin, Eloquent Essayist in Behalf of Civil Rights, is Dead." *New York Times,* December 2, 1987, p. 1.

Daniels, Lee A. "James Baldwin, the Writer, Dies in France at 63." *New York Times,* December 1, 1987, p. D27.

Darrach, Brad. "James Baldwin, A Manchild from Harlem, Sang the Song of Himself with a Fury that Seared Us All." *People Weekly,* December 21, 1987, p. 89.

Friedman, Otto. "Bearing Witness to the Truth: James Baldwin: 1924–1987." *Time* 130 (December 14, 1987): 80

Hart, Jeffrey. "James Baldwin RIP." *National Review* 39 (December 1987): 17.

Meisler, Stanley. "Baldwin Dies at 63." *Los Angeles Times,* December 2, 1987, p. 1.

Obituary. *Jet* 73 (December 1987): 14.

Obituary. *Nation* 245 (December 1987): 740.

Obituary. *New York Times,* December 2, 1987, p. 30.

Obituary. *Los Angeles Times,* December 2, 1987, p. 6.

Pinckney, Darryl. "On James Baldwin (1924–1987)." *New York Review of Books* 34 (January 1988): 8.

Prescott, Peter S. "The Dilemma of a Native Son: James Baldwin Was Our Black Jeremiah." *Newsweek* 110 (December 14, 1987): 86.

Sanchez, Sonia. "A Remembrance." *Essence* 18 (March 1988): 52.

Troupe, Quincy. "The Last Interview." *Essence* 18 (March 1988): 53.

Washington, Elsie B. "James Baldwin, 1924–1987: A Tribute." *Essence* 18 (March 1988): 51.

Wilkins, Roger. "Baldwin On My Mind." *Washington Post,* December 5, 1987, p. A27.

Williams, John A. "The Demise of a Conscience in 1987." *Los Angeles Times,* December 26, 1987, p. 8

INDEX

ABOUT THE AUTHOR

Horace Porter is associate professor of English and chair of African and Afro-American studies at Dartmouth College. A graduate of Amherst College (B.A., 1972), Porter received a Ph.D. (1981) from Yale. This is his first book. He has written for *Washington Post Book World*, *The American Scholar*, *Change*, *The Journal of Negro History*, and *Obsidion*. His home is in Hanover, New Hampshire. In 1988–89 he is a visiting professor of English at University College, London.

ABOUT THE BOOK

Stealing the Fire was composed on the Mergenthaler 202 in Galliard, a contemporary rendering of a classic typeface prepared for Mergenthaler in 1978 by the British type designer Matthew Carter. The book was composed by Brevis Press, Bethany, Connecticut, and designed and produced by Kachergis Book Design, Pittsboro, North Carolina.

WESLEYAN UNIVERSITY PRESS, 1989